EVEN SO SEND I YOU

EVEN SO
SEND I YOU

COR BRUINS

CHAPTER TWO
PLUMSTEAD, LONDON

© 1985 Chapter Two, Plumstead, London SE18 3EX, England

1st British edition 1986

Translated from the Dutch edition ,, . . . zo zend ik ook u'' published
1981 by Uitgeverij H. Medema, Apeldoorn 7300.
Also translated into French and German.

ISBN 0 947588 08 6

Bible quotations taken from the Authorized Version (Crown copyright)
and the New Translation of J. N. Darby.

Distributors:
Australia & New Zealand: Geelong Christian Literature,
110 Barwon Blvd., Highton, Victoria 3216, Australia.
Canada: Believers Bookshelf Inc, 430 Victoria Street,
Niagara on the Lake, Ontario LOS 1 JO, Canada.
Eire & Northern Ireland: Words of Truth, PO Box 147,
Belfast BT8 47T, Northern Ireland.
England & Scotland: Central Bible Hammond Trust Ltd,
30 South Road, Wooler, Northumberland NE71 6SP.
United States of America: Believers Bookshelf Inc, Box 261,
Sunbury, Pennsylvania 17801, USA.

Production: Rodney P Shepherd
Cover design: Tony Cantale Graphics

Designed and printed in Great Britain for
CHAPTER TWO
95 Genesta Road, Plumstead, London SE18 3EX by
Nuprint Services Ltd, Harpenden, Herts AL5 4SE

CONTENTS

Foreword   7

Part One: The pattern Jesus – our example

  1 What's it all about?   11
  2 The uniqueness of Christ   14

Part Two: The preparation – a life that God will use

  3 In the school of God   33
  4 Abraham – willing to give up his rights   37
  5 Moses – the meekest servant of God   63
  6 Paul – the greatest missionary of all times   83

Part Three: The person in question – you!

  7 God is calling *you*   139
  8 How do I know that I'm called?   151

FOREWORD

Have you ever wondered if you have been called to serve the Lord? If you know Him as your Saviour and Lord then undoubtedly the matter of service has arisen. The Lord has not left us as rudderless ships, He has given us His Word and the Holy Spirit. This book directs the reader to the Scriptures for the guidance we need.

It is not a theoretical study: the author has experienced much in the Lord's service and his object is to encourage us in a real experimental relationship with God. If we yield, without reserve, our lives to the Lord we will see that our God has not changed, He can still do wonderful things today. Neither is this book intended for the theorist. It is the prayer of author and publisher alike that the contents will not merely be armchair reading but be put into practice in the reality of a life in communion with Christ. The reader ought not to expect a thorough exegesis of the lives of Abraham, Moses and Paul but rather see the strands of thought their lives suggest, which may serve to indicate how the Lord would send us. The many personal references of the author have the same object. Of course the experiences are not blue-prints for others. The standard in all things must be the Scriptures, but it is helpful to see in these examples how the Lord can work.

We leave this book in the Lord's hands, without whose blessing all man's work is fruitless, praying that He may use these pages in the lives of His own to do His will.

Edwin Cross

PART ONE

THE PATTERN JESUS – OUR EXAMPLE

1

WHAT'S IT ALL ABOUT?

He was sent

In His prayer in John 17:18 the Lord Jesus, speaking of His disciples, says to His Father 'As thou hast sent me into the world, even so have I also sent them into the world'.

The word *sent* in this verse is the twice repeated Greek word *apostello*. This word has the meaning of sending an envoy authoritatively. The Lord uses this same word in: Matthew 10:16 Mark 11:1; Luke 22:8; John 4:38; on each occasion He addresses the apostles. We can therefore safely conclude that the word *apostello* refers to the sending of someone with an official message.

He wants to send us

In John 20:21 we read; 'Then said Jesus to them again, Peace be unto you: *as* my Father hath sent me, *even so send I you*'. When the Lord speaks of the fact that the Father has sent Him, He again uses the word *apostello,* but when He speaks to His disciples He uses the other word for sending: *pempo*, which is a more general term which simply denotes the *relation* of the one who sends and the one who is sent. This last sending forth is the outflow of a conscious and intimate existing relationship which in the Scriptures always precedes the sending with an official message.

In Mark 3;14 we find this beautifully illustrated: 'And he ordained twelve, that they *should be with him*, and that he might *send them forth*'. The Holy Spirit clearly emphasizes that our personal relationship with Jesus Christ, or in other words, what He is to us, and what we are to Him, precedes what we *do* for Him! In our experience this order is often reversed! We are so often occupied in service for Him, that we neglect the most essential – spending much time with Him.

In the Old Testament we see this same principle applied in the service of the priests and Levites. Applied to ourselves this of course does not mean that the priest and the Levite are two different persons. But the priestly element in us must take precedence over the Levitical element, and in fact ought to give direction to it. A clear illustration of this is found in the case of Epaphras. We read in Colossians 1:7; 'As ye also learned of Epaphras our dear fellow servant, who is for you a faithful minister of Christ'. Here we find the Levitical element in the service and the priestly element in chapter 4:12 where we read: 'Epaphras, who is one of you, a servant of Christ...always labouring fervently for you in prayers...'.

So on the one hand we see what the Spirit of God seeks to work in us, and on the other hand what we, in dependence upon that same Spirit, must work out.

It must be perfectly clear to us all that no believer is exempt from the workings of the Spirit either in him or through him. The question is: how many of us allow the Holy Spirit free course to work in us to conform us to the image of Christ? He longs for us to be able to taste that sweet communion with Christ, and to be obedient to His will.

How many of us have really totally abandoned ourselves to the Lord Jesus Christ, so that now He can do with us what He pleases? Is that really your desire, brother and sister? Do you know the Lord Jesus personally and intimately? I do not mean whether He is your Saviour, I take that for granted, for you would not otherwise want to read this book. But what I mean is whether Jesus Christ is your Lord and Master? Remember, 'If He is not Lord of all, then He is not Lord at all'.

My purpose with the first part of this book is that together we reflect upon this question: what is in fact our true and real relationship to Jesus Christ? You will have remarked that in the verses quoted from the Gospel of John, we have twice repeated the comparative form: 'As...even so' (John 17:18; 20:21). As the Father sent the Son, even so the Son would send His disciples. In other words the sending forth of the disciples would be patterned after, or similar to, the sending of the Son by the Father.

Just as Jesus Christ's relationship to the Father was one of deepest intimacy and total submission to His will, even so must all that we are and do be patterned after the divine model. This is a fundamental principle which we neglect at our own peril and loss. There is nothing more important in your and my life than the maintenance of our relationship with our Lord Jesus Christ unspoilt and uninterrupted. We must therefore daily cultivate this communion with Him, by meditating in His presence; and so that we might follow His example, by asking ourselves, how did Christ live for His Father on earth? How was He sent?

2

THE UNIQUENESS OF CHRIST

By this we mean the consciousness which the Lord Jesus had that He was here on earth not for His own personal interests, but for the interests of His Father. This consciousness He expresses in John 8:29 'I do always those things that please him.'

Let us pause here for a moment. If the Lord Jesus is to be our model, have we been obedient to this first and fundamental requirement: that we are where we are, for Him only? Why are the Communists so successful? Because they are totally committed to their ideal. Why are the Muslims and other spurious movements so successful? Because their adherents are obsessed with what they believe. In society, those who are successful, and at the top of the ladder, who are specialists in their field, are those who are 'sold out' in utter abandonment to achieve their goal.

Jesus Christ said: 'Lo, I come . . . to do thy will, O God' (Heb 10:7) – not His own will, but the Father's will. Brother, sister, is this a reality in our lives? Is to do the will of Christ more essential to us than anything else? If not, then it is no wonder that there is no fruit for God in our lives, that we are so little like our Lord Jesus. We are busy perhaps here and there, even in service for Him, but there is no fruit. We must therefore begin by asking the Lord to give us this 'sense of mission', this realisation that we are here for Him, and not for ourselves.

His calling

In Colossians 1:15 we read of Jesus Christ that He is 'the image of the invisible God...'. The meaning of the word image is 'representation' (not 'likeness', for Christ is not inferior, but on equal terms in the Godhead). Jesus Christ came to represent His Father, but also to 'manifest' the invisible God. He came, so to speak, to make the invisible visible. He shone out with God's glory. He came to glorify God in this world where God had been outraged and rebelled against.

The reason for His mission is simply that He 'was sent'. More than 40 times in the Gospel of John we read that the Son, Jesus Christ, is referred to as the 'Sent One'. Amongst the many other reasons we could mention why the Lord Jesus came, it will suffice to mention only the following: He came to call sinners (Luke 5:32, compare with Rom 3:23); He came not to judge but to save (John 12:47, compare with Luke 19:10); to bear witness to the truth (John 18:37, compare with 1 John 5:19); to accept the bitter cup (John 12:27, compare with Ps 116:13); He came to minister and not to be ministered unto (Matt 20:28); He came to give His life a ransom (Matt 20:28, compare with Ps 49:7).

Again the challenge comes to us all at this stage whether we are willing to follow Him. Is it also our aim to make God known to others, and to glorify God in hostile surroundings, and to show the love of God in calling, speaking, witnessing, serving and giving ourselves to others? (1 John 3:16). This is indeed the reason why the Lord, the moment He saved us, did not take us straight to heaven, but gave us a 'mission', and the reason for that mission. Can we say like the apostle Paul:

'. . . I was not disobedient . . .'? (Acts 26:19).

As there are many facets to a diamond, so it is with the object of Christ's calling. Perhaps we could say that one of the facets was others – the salvation, blessing, happiness and peace of others.

He came to the Jews first, but there were also those 'others' (John 10:16) – not that they wanted Him, or that they were waiting to receive Him with open arms. If our object is anything other than to be in His hands to do with as He pleases, we shall be deeply disillusioned. If we think we are going to be really appreciated by those whom we think need us, we are going to be very much disappointed. If we make our primary object a work for Jesus, a ministry, a specific country or anything else, we have not understood that the Spirit's primary object for us is to be utterly devoted to Jesus Christ. Out of that devotion to Him will grow a comprehension of what and where He wants us to be for Him. Some keen believers make the missionfield their primary object. Others may think that service in the home-country must be their object. The fact is that we must make nothing an object in itself.

We are often amazed at seeing the apparent wastefulness of God with regard to His evaluation of the servant and his service. Paul says that God 'hath chosen the foolish things of the world to confound the wise; and God hath chosen the weak things of the world to confound the things which are mighty' (1 Cor 1:27). God has a totally 'other' evaluation from ourselves. We look at a person, a servant of God, and evaluate his usefulness and effectiveness according to how talented he is, what he has and what he has not. God evaluates the inner man. For instance recently a brother said to me that he could not understand why I 'wasted my knowledge of Arabic'. He felt that because I know Arabic, it was only logical that my field of service should be the Arabic speaking world. Is this the way the Lord evaluates?

Personally I do not think so necessarily. I know for instance a missionary of Swiss nationality who is currently serving God on an English speaking missionfield, and I have a friend, born in England, who has served God for the last 30 years in the French speaking world.

A God-given ability must never become an object in itself, not even in relation to the service of God. God's aim may simply be to use the process through which we have had to go to develop that special ability, and He may eventually not even use that particular ability. But He will have used the process of developing the ability in the formation of moral and spiritual character: the need for patience, perseverance, a willingness to sacrifice, etc. When He has reached His purpose with us, He may simply 'waste' what to us seems so essential and vital for His service.

God's ways are not stereotyped: 'For my thoughts are not your thoughts, neither are your ways my ways, saith the Lord' (see Isa 55:8,9). Your and my primary goal should be HIM. The detail as to where He wants us will be ultimately shown and become clear to us. Our being made to conform to His image is of greater importance to Him than what we do for Him. So then, if He is really our only object we shall not be hurt or too much disappointed when we are not appreciated or accepted, either by our fellow-believers, or by a hostile world which does not want Christ.

When Jesus Christ is our object, we shall be characterised by a spirit which calmly evaluates things before Him, and does not pretend to do great things, but according to the circumstances we will adapt ourselves and our service and continue on our way with Him happily. In this pathway of walking with Jesus, He will bring people across our way – needy people, sinful people. We did not choose them. He did. We have no special sympathies. Christ Jesus will often, unconsciously to ourselves, minister to others through us.

The object of the Lord Jesus was always to have the Father's approval and the Holy Spirit's direction. That is how He went about among the masses, amongst His friends and acquaintances, and touched and transformed lives. His object was always to be where His Father wanted Him, and He never acted independently of His Father (John 8:28).

His authority

The Lord Jesus says in John 7:28: 'I am not come of myself, but he that sent me is true...' The authority for His mission was the fact that He knew that He was sent by the Father. This is a fundamental principle which all who are engaged in some form of service for the Lord must consider. Has He sent you? Can you speak with *His* authority? Never begin any activity for the Lord unless you are absolutely sure that He has sent you to do that specific thing. In Hebrews 5:4 we find a serious warning in relation to this: '...no man taketh this honour unto himself, but he that is *called of God*'. Sincerity and zeal are no substitutes for that authority which is essential to any service for the Lord whether at home or abroad. That authority is the Word of God, the revelation of God's will and mind.

Moses went with the authority of 'I am that I am', (Ex 3:14). Gideon was told: 'Go in this thy might... have not I sent thee?' (Jud 6:14). David could say: 'I come to thee in the name of the Lord of hosts...' (1 Sam 17:45). Later on he forgot this necessity for dependence upon the Lord for everything he did. In 2 Samuel 6 for instance we see his zeal and sincerity to please the Lord, but these otherwise splendid virtues are no substitute for real God-given authority. David's desire was admirable: he would not give sleep to his eyes until he had found a place for the Lord's ark (Ps 132:4). But God could not approve of the way David went about bringing the ark back. The whole project ended in disaster and sorrow. Let us learn a lesson from this incident, that God's work must always be done according to God's mind.

You may feel you are called for instance to China or to Brazil, or to go full-time in the Lord's work at home. But remember that although this conviction may be crystal clear to you, it will nevertheless have to go through the purifying fire of testing, to prove both to yourself as well as to others, your brothers and sisters in Christ, that you have the authority and approval of God. Moses had to wait 40 years for this. You and I may have to wait. God may ask you even to put that call of yours on the altar of sacrifice.

All our motives must go through death, even our personal desire to serve the Lord. But if we are ready to accept that, then He will bring us through to resurrection. It will then no longer be just *my* or *your* desire, but a purified and more intense longing to be utterly for Him, and to do only that which He wishes. Paul says: 'Truly the signs of an apostle were wrought among you....' (2 Cor 12:12). An apostle was one sent with authority: the signs and miracles proved it. There is still today, in of course a much lesser degree since we are not apostles like the apostle Paul, the necessity for this token of God's approval upon a servant.

His motives

It was love for His Father which made the Lord Jesus say: 'Lo, I come...to do thy will, O God' (Heb 10:7).

It was the mutual love of the Father for the Son and the Son for the Father that energized, so to speak, all that Christ did. 'As the Father knoweth me, even so know I the Father: and I lay down my life for the sheep... Therefore doth my Father love me, because I lay down my life....' (John 10:15, 17). 'Hereby perceive we the love, because he laid down his life for us: and we ought to lay down our lives for the brethren' (1 John 3:16). The all-pervading motive of all that Christ did and said was this self-sacrificing love to the Father. It was that love that made Him lay aside His glory, that caused Him to make Himself of no reputation, that made him take upon Himself the form of a servant, that made Him humble Himself, and become obedient unto death, even the death of the Cross.

Nothing less than these qualities of self-sacrificing love must be the prime motive of our service for Christ. He has given us the example: 'Let this mind be in you'. This love is the spontaneous outgoing of my heart and affections to Him. Paul says: '...the love of Christ constraineth us...' (2 Cor 5:14). That love was the great motive of all His service.

In this fifth chapter of 2 Corinthians we find still further motives for ourselves:

1. The fact that God has prepared indescribable future blessedness for us in heaven (v.1).
2. The fact that God has given us already now the earnest of the Spirit (v.5).
3. The fact that we want to be agreeable to Him (v.9).
4. The fact that we must all be made manifest at the judgment seat of Christ. And could we bear the thought of coming empty-handed? (v.10).
5. The fact that we know the terror of the Lord (v.11).
6. The fact that we who are alive in Him should not henceforth live unto ourselves, but unto Him who died for us, and rose again (v.15).
7. The fact that we are ambassadors for Christ (v.20).

All these are ingredients of the motive that should make our hearts respond to His great love. This is the only worthy and valid motive for true service!

His message

Nicodemus acknowledged that Jesus was a teacher 'come from God' (John 3:2). And 'all bare him witness and wondered at the gracious words which proceeded out of his mouth' (Luke 4:22). Even his enemies had to confess: 'Never man spake like this man' (John 7:46).

Basically His message was one of *forgiveness* and *hope*.

a. Of *forgiveness*: His great themes were the fact of the unbearable burden of human sin, and the super abounding divine mercy and grace. He called the weary to receive His peace of mind and rest of soul. He brought the message of free and full forgiveness to sin-stricken hearts. That is the reason why 'the common people heard Him gladly' (Mark 12:37), and that multitudes of sinners flocked to hear Him (Luke 15:1)

b. Of *hope*: He alone could rightly understand the value of a human soul and discern the potential of a forgiven sinner. That is why He taught saying: 'How much then is a man better than a sheep?' (Matt 12:12). Yes, He offered hope for the worst of sinners, and promised strength for the feeblest.

His message was also:

1. *Universal* in its appeal and application. It was suited to all, whether adults or children. It has a never fading appeal at all times, throughout all the ages, and not merely for the age in which He lived. It still calls for repentance and trust.

2. *Complete*: Because it touches life at every point, from the regulation of the thoughts and motives, to the control of the will and conduct. It emphasizes humility, and refuses the satisfaction of any personal interest.

3. *Permanent*: Not many of the great thinkers of this world would set aside His teaching as irrelevant and obsolete.

4. *Authoritative*: It was with absolute and incontestable authority that He spoke. There was a sureness and absence of doubt and hesitation about everthing He said. He had no need to recall, correct, modify or safeguard anything He said. No one could find any fault in what He actually said. His words carried conviction even in the face of strong opposition. He could not be gainsaid because it was too evident that He actually lived all that He taught.

5. *Inexhaustible*: Generation after generation finds in it what is new, fresh and inspiring (Matt 24:35).

6. *Verifiable*: He invited anyone to verify for himself whether what He said was true: 'If any man will do his will, he shall know of the doctrine, whether it be of God, or whether I speak of myself' (John 7:17). Wisdom is justified of her children (Matt 11:19), and His words verified themselves in human lives, because they possess a dynamic and a special and unique power that transforms the hearts and lives of men and women.

7. *Original*: Because of its divine origin. Jesus Christ associated His teaching with Himself. He connected the Kingdom with Himself as King. He linked the Fatherhood of God with Himself as the unique revealer (Matt 11:27). He associated forgiveness with His own prerogative and authority (Mark 2:10). There is no word of His teaching which He does not in some way make to depend on Himself.

To sum up, we see Him as:
Prophet: He reveals God to man.
Priest: He redeems man and leads him into God's Presence.
King: He rules and judges mankind.
These aspects constitute His mission, and each point is found in His teaching.
He is Himself the real theme of His teaching. Jesus

Christ is Himself the truth, and is at once the subject of His teaching and the medium through whom the truth is to be perceived and received. (see John 8:25). It is simply impossible to accept the teaching without acknowledging the claims of the teacher. Jesus Christ came not to preach the Gospel, but that there might be a Gospel to preach. It is the Gospel which *He* Himself *is* rather than anything He ever taught, that constitutes Christianity.

It is not only essential that we *have* a message, but that we *are* the message we preach. We cannot be dissociated from the message we carry to a lost mankind. It is Christ living in us that is the message. We must preach Christ, not ourselves. Philip in Acts 8:5 '...went down to the city of Samaria, and *preached Christ* unto them', and later as he met with the Ethiopian eunuch, we read: 'Philip opened his mouth, and began at the same scripture, and preached unto him *Jesus*'(v.35). Paul says: '...our gospel came not to you in word only, but also in power, and in the Holy Ghost, and in much assurance' (1 Thess 1:5).

His character

All Christ's ministry was characterised by humility: 'I am meek and lowly in heart...' (Matt 11:29). He, the Creator of the universe who was served and worshipped by myriads of angels, said of Himself: 'the Son of man came not to be ministered unto, but to minister, and to give his life a ransom for many' (Matt 20:28).

As the Master, so must the servant be. We can never be really effective for Christ if we have a spirit of superiority. Like Ezekiel we must sit where they, to whom we are sent, sit (Ezek 3:15). He was filled with a holy *zeal* for God (John 2:17) and was filled with *courage* and great *determination*. 'He stedfastly set his face to go to Jerusalem...' (Luke 9:51). The apostle Paul later followed in his master's footsteps (Acts 20:24).

But Christ's determination had its roots in *utter depen-*
dence upon His Father. He always acted in absolute
harmony with His Father's will. Of course He was criticised by the unregenerate men who could not understand
why one moment He said: 'I go not up yet unto this
feast...', and then later '...when his brethren were
gone up, then went He also up unto the feast' (John
7:8,10). Glorious and holy 'inconsistency'!

So it must also be with the spiritual believer who
'judgeth all things, yet he himself is judged of no man' (1
Cor 2:15). The believer can evaluate others, by spiritual
discernment, but unbelievers do not understand him.
His motives and actions seem inexplicable to them
because he lives 'in a different world'. If we try to please
men, we will not please God. Therefore let us lay all
criticism at His feet as we walk with Him.

The Lord Jesus also showed utter *self-denial* in never
seeking His own comfort, or to please Himself (John
8:50). Many servants of Christ on the foreign missionfield
have not always put into practice what Christ said of
Himself: '...the Son of man hath not where to lay his
head...'. Many have brought along with them their own
culture, and have thus isolated themselves from the very
people they came to serve.

Although Himself perfect, Jesus could nevertheless
appreciate what others did that must have been very
imperfect to Him (Mary in John 12; the rich young ruler
in Mark 10:21). The poor and the weak and the defence-
less had a great champion in Him. How kind and friendly
He was with little children. How they loved Him! All
these virtues must also characterise us if the Lord is
going to send us on a mission whether at home or abroad.
Anyone who is not ready and willing to be so transformed
into His image is unfit for His service.

His prayer-life

If the Son of God found prayer necessary in His life, what place do you think it ought to have in ours? His disciples, who never asked to be taught how to preach, begged Him that He would teach them how to pray.

When was it the disciples asked Jesus to teach them to pray? – 'as he was praying in a certain place...' (Luke 11:1). Was it then primarily His example they felt was a part of the pattern they should follow? Was it because of an awakening spiritual life and the yearning and craving after fellowship with God? Was it because they felt they could trace the evident power and effectiveness of Jesus' life and ministry – His graciousness and gentleness, His love and tenderness, His wisdom and meekness, His truth and genuineness – back to Jesus' prayer-life as their fountainhead? Was it an undefined sense of need which they instinctively felt could be met only by a life of prayer such as they saw in the Saviour?

The four Gospels together give us a marvellous picture of Jesus' prayer-life. In Luke's Gospel, where the Holy Spirit shows us Jesus as the Perfect Man, we see Him more than in any other Gospel also as the dependent Man. On at least seven different occasions we find Jesus Christ praying (Luke 3:21; 5:16; 6:12; 9:18; 28; 11:1; 22:41–44).

We see Jesus praying at His baptism (Luke 3:22), and also after He had healed many sick (Mark 1:35). When His fame began to spread and people came flocking to hear Him preach, He prays (Luke 5:16). Before appointing His disciples we find Him in prayer for guidance (Luke 6:12). After He fed the 5000 He prays. (Mark 6:46). Before telling His disciples of His coming sufferings, He prays (Luke 9:18). Then, while He was being transfigured before the eyes of His three disciples, He is seen praying (Luke 9:28). Before going to raise Lazarus, He prays (John 11:41), and before He taught

His disciples to pray, He was found of them as He was praying (Luke 11:1). When His soul was troubled, He prayed (John 12:27), and when He was about to leave his disciples, He prayed (John 17). The night before His death in the Garden of Gethsemane we find Him in agonising prayer. And finally He died praying while hanging on the cross (Matt 26:36; Luke 23: 34,46).

Jesus Christ lived a life of prayer. Yet we do not see Him all the time on His knees. There was never a more active man than Jesus Christ. Several times we read that He spent the whole night praying, or that He was on His knees a great while before the day dawned.

The Lord Jesus shows us in all this that in the lives of those who follow Him there must be set times and a known place for prayer. Here we see our great need for a disciplined life. Disorganised Christians are usually prayerless Christians. In order to pray we must be willing to sacrifice, perhaps to take time early in the morning or at night.

Whilst praying we need to discipline our mind and thoughts not to wander but to concentrate on our prayer. Prayer is first of all communion, although it also takes the form of supplication, intercession, praise and thanksgiving.

Prayer is the occupation of the soul with its *needs*.

Praise is the occupation of the soul with its *blessings*.

Worship is the occupation of the soul with *God*.

The mature believer must know the practical reality of all these exercises in his own daily life before he can ever be effective as a servant. Have we learned the secret of a life of prayer? Remember: without breathing there is no life; without praying there is no power.

His preaching

Those who heard Jesus said of Him: 'Never man spake like this man' (John 7:46). Grace was poured into His lips. (Ps 45).

Sherwood Eddy in his book 'A portrait for Jesus', says: 'Jesus left no book, no tract or written page behind him. He bequeathed no system, no philosophy, no theology, no legislation. He raised no armies, organised no institutions, held no office, sought no influence. He was no scholar, and yet He is more quoted than any writer in all history. His sayings at times are almost on every tongue, and His words have literally gone out into all the world. No man ever laid down his life in Asia or Africa to translate Plato or Aristotle, Kant or Hegel, Shakespeare or Milton, but hundreds have died to carry Jesus' priceless words to the ends of the earth. Several hundred languages have been reduced to writing in order to transmit His life-giving message. Savage tribes have been uplifted, cannibals civilised, head-hunters converted, schools and colleges founded, and the character and culture of individuals and of peoples have been changed as the result of the influence of His words which are creative spirit and life. His discourses (almost 50), sermons and utterances, contain His teaching for the saints of all ages. The substance of His teaching covers a wide variety of themes. Yet all the recorded words of Christ could be printed in a 16 page pamphlet. His longest speech takes but 15 minutes to read aloud! According as the occasions presented themselves He adapted His teachings: sometimes parabolic, or allegoric, sometimes polemical or didactic. He as persuasive in His manner and tone. His words and preaching were remarkable for their brevity, beauty, purity, sympathy, wonder, prophetic value and dignity'.

What a pattern for us to follow! The apostle Paul exhorts us: 'Let your speech be always with grace, seasoned with salt, that ye may know how ye ought to answer every man' (Col 4:6).

His methods

John 4 gives us a wonderful example of the way in which our Lord Jesus acted. Here we have what we might call: 'Seven steps in soul-winning'.

Step 1: Jesus establishes contact (v.7). He does this in such a humble and gracious way, and with such infinite tact. Our Lord puts Himself in the woman's *debt* before He offers her *a gift* in return. He will condescend to drink of our *pitcher* to encourage us to drink of His *fountain*.

Step 2: Jesus arouses her interest: (v.10). 'If thou knewest'. He implied that He knew something she did not know. She becomes curious! Here is the ability to turn a casual meeting into an occasion of highest spiritual significance in which men and women are brought face to face with Christ.

Step 3: Jesus creates a desire (v.14). Having gained her confidence and roused her curiosity, Jesus now discloses His real message: the gift of living water.

Step 4: Jesus shifts the attention to spiritual needs: (v.16). This is to awaken her to her own need and to make her face up to her sinful condition.

Step 5: Jesus compels her to face up to reality (vv. 17,18). He faces her with the problem of personal sin: 'Go call your husband'. She replies: 'I have no husband', and is still evasive. She gives the impression that she might still be a widow or unmarried or divorced. So Jesus must therefore now expose her sin.

Step 6: Jesus presents the hard facts (vv. 21–24). He cannot allow her any longer to hide herself.

Step 7: Jesus reveals Himself to her as Saviour (v.26): 'I that speak unto thee am he'. Jesus declares His Messiahship openly to the woman because she was ready to receive Him and wanted what He offered. Many of us know the *facts* of the Gospel, but that is not sufficient; we must also know how to *present* them, so that we might win souls for Christ.

A Christian barber had been to a meeting one night and came away deeply convicted of his own lack of zeal to win souls for the Lord Jesus. He decided that this must change, and that he would speak of the Lord Jesus to the first customer next morning. He had just finished soaping his customer and was now sharpening his razor on the leather. Turning to the man in the chair and waving his sharpened razor he said to him: 'Well, sir, are you ready to die and pass into eternity?' We may laugh at this story, but it is a tragic example of complete tactlessness in presenting Christ to the unsaved.

There are people with whom we may come in contact for whom the Lord does not give us a message at that particular moment. It is not God's purpose either that we feel under compulsion to speak to every person we happen to meet. Otherwise the winning of souls would become a veritable bondage. But God does expect us always to be willing to speak with every one. Let us remember the words of our gracious Lord Jesus in John 13:15,16 'I have given you an example that ye should do as I have done to you. Verily, verily, I say unto you, the servant is not greater than his lord, neither he that is sent greater than he that sent him'.

Someone once passed on the following interesting advice for those who desire to win souls for Christ:

1. Never get side-tracked into an argument.
2. Learn to listen; give the other one a chance to say something.
3. As a rule speak to those of your own sex.
4. It is better not to counsel anyone much older than yourself.
5. Do not trust your own ability.
6. Do not pour forth whole strings of texts and scriptures and host of illustrations; three or four scripture references are quite sufficient.

7. Do not become impatient.
8. Do not become discouraged if you do not have immediate success.

PART TWO

THE PREPARATION
– A LIFE THAT
GOD WILL USE

3

IN THE
SCHOOL OF GOD

In the first part of this book we have seen that Jesus
Christ is our pattern, and that His virtues and His mind
must be found in us also. This is God's plan for all of us
without exception. The Holy Spirit as the divine *teacher*
in the school of God seeks to conform us to the image of
Christ, and to transform our lives. As the divine Weaver
He sits daily before the loom of our lives, with the
pattern of Christ in front of Him. By the knotting and
cutting of the wool He seeks to realise the pattern in the
ever growing fabric of the carpet of our lives on His
loom. This knotting and cutting in our lives is undoubtedly a painful process. It is through suffering that we are
purified like gold in the crucible. The self-life within us
must also practically be brought into death with Jesus
Christ. We have to learn to say in all the daily circumstances of our lives: 'Not I, but Christ'. This is not an
easy thing.

We can see the application of this principle also in the
lives of men of God in the Old Testament. Abraham did
not become the 'friend of God' overnight. It was the
culmination of spending years in the school of God.
Every day he had to learn to say 'no' to his own inclina-

tions, and 'yes' to God. This was the way in which Abraham learned to discern the will of God in his daily experience. This is also the way in which we, each one of us personally, have to learn to discern the will of God for our lives. He who calls us to follow Him, is the same who before He sends us out into the world, teaches us first of all to understand his thoughts and His ways.

No one has the right to go out or to do something for the Lord Jesus, unless he has been sent by Him. Jesus Christ alone has this right to send. No organisation, no mission-board or committee has this right to send. The Lord will not send anyone without due preparation and qualification, and this preparatory process takes place daily in our fellowship with the Lord. There will never be a moment when we can do without this. No-one can ever say in this life: 'I have finished my training and preparation in the school of God; now I know all there is to know.'

It seems that in the Old Testament we find a kind of period of apprenticeship in the qualifying of the young priest. If we compare Numbers 4:3 with 8:23–26, we discover that from the age of 25 to 30 years there is this period of apprenticeship. This seems to teach us that in God's thoughts the capability of His servants is developed *whilst* they serve.

In the New Testament we also see this principle applied in the case of Barnabus and Saul, in Acts 13, to which we will return later.

Young believers should for instance be encouraged to make a start with preparation by regularly attending the weekly prayer-meeting, where they can *learn* to pray, eventually in public. The older believers ought to be living examples to them in this spiritual exercise. Perhaps it is good here to emphasize the very serious responsibility of the older believers. The writer has known cases in which younger brethren expressed themselves in the prayer-meeting in perhaps a rather unconventional way, or somewhat imperfectly, hesitatingly and simply, which is of course quite normal for beginners. But the fact that they were beginners and young and inexperienced was over-looked by their elder brethren. An older brother felt that the title 'Lord', or 'Lord Jesus' was far too often repeated in a young brother's prayer. He told him therefore that he ought not to do this. Other examples could be cited. The result was that the young brother became so afraid that he might make a mistake in the prayer-meeting, that he stopped praying altogether. There are today brothers in the assemblies of believers who never open their mouths either in praise or in prayer or in any other spiritual exercise as the result of an unfortunate, unkind or tactless remark of a brother in the past.

A similarly serious responsibility rests with the elder brethren with regard the weekly Bible-study. The needs of our younger brothers and sisters in Christ ought to be kept well in mind, and the Bible-study ought to be spiritual and interesting so that young people will be keen to attend regularly. The training-school for would-be servants of the Lord should ideally be the local assembly of believers.

There are activities for which no very great gift is needed and in which keen young believers could be engaged. Visiting the sick and infirm, helping in the Sunday-school, or youth group, distributing tracts, open-air preaching etc. As they allow themselves to be led by the Holy Spirit in these activities, young believers find that the process of spiritual preparation develops and continues quietly. They will thus be qualified by the Spirit to do further service for the Lord as He appoints.

If at the age of 25 we are not conscious of the necessity for this process of preparation by God's Spirit, when we reach the age of 30 we will certainly not be spiritually qualified to do any responsible service either amongst believers or outside in the world. What we eventually will be doing for the Lord somewhere, is simply the outflow and result of our daily learning in the school of God.

Let us then continue to illustrate these principles from the experiences of Abraham.

4

ABRAHAM – WILLINGNESS TO GIVE UP MY OWN RIGHTS

Unquestioning obedience (Genesis 11:27–32)

God's call had come to Abram in Ur of the Chaldees, as Genesis 12:1 seems to indicate: 'Now the Lord *had* said unto Abram'. But Abram had only partially obeyed God's call, which was: 'Get thee out of thy country, and from thy *kindred*, and from thy father's house, unto a land that I will shew thee'. (See also Acts 7:2).

God will never accept half-measures, or compromises. Incomplete obedience is really disobedience. The terms of God's call were quite clear: 'Get thee out from thy kindred and thy father's house...'. But we now read: 'And Terah took Abram his son...and they came unto Haran, and *dwelt* there'. Well, had he not left Ur of the Chaldees? Yes, but his father, and part of his kindred were still with him. And we might even say that he were still with his father. Now they had stopped at Haran to dwell there. This was definitely not the land that God would show him. How then could Abram be content to dwell there? Just as Abram had to learn unquestioning and total obedience, so must you and I.

In this section we would like to discuss the call of the Lord Jesus. This call comes to all of us without distinction. He calls us to come to Him as Saviour and

Redeemer, that He might deliver us from the burden of sin and that we may find rest (Matt 11:28). How few there are who realise the further call of the Lord Jesus in order that they might follow Him daily as His disciples: 'Take my yoke upon you, and learn of me; for I am meek and lowly in heart: and ye shall find rest unto your souls' (Matt 11:29). He does not only want to be our Saviour but also Lord of our lives.

Let me share with you a little of how in my experience I realised that He was calling me. Although I was brought up in a fine Christian home by faithful and godly parents and consequently knew the Good Shepherd from my earliest childhood, I did not have the experience of the joy of knowing that all my sins were forgiven and the assurance of salvation until the age of seventeen. I had this personal encounter with the Lord Jesus Christ on a Sunday afternoon in 1947. The Holy Spirit did not only convict me of the sinful deeds I had done, but also that I was a helpless sinner and needed salvation. When I confessed my sins I found Him faithful and just for He forgave me all my sins and cleansed me from all un-righteousness (1 John 1:9). What joy and peace flooded my soul! I wanted everybody to know my Saviour also. When therefore a brother invited me to come and help in the Sunday-school in the Hague (where I lived), I was glad to respond.

I had never been taught the necessity of having a daily 'quiet time'; to set aside a period for regular systematic bible-reading and prayer. When this was pointed out to me a whole new world opened up for me. What comfort and encouragement I found daily in the Word of God. I began to grow spiritually and learned to bring everything to the Lord in prayer. I learned through the Bible to look for guidance, joy began to flood my life and I began to realise that I must share my new-found wealth with others.

By the way, many young people have asked me

what is the best way to read the Bible so they might really get blessing from their reading. Here are a few tips about how to have blessed times with your Bible, which we in our large family have often put into practice with blessed results:

Before you open your Bible, pray for help and guidance from the Lord. Ask Him to open your spiritual understanding so you may know His will and obey it.

Read regularly and systematically through the Bible, perhaps every day, morning and evening, a portion in the Old Testament and in the New Testament. There are many excellent plans of readings from Genesis to Revelation available spread over one to five years which you can get in evangelical bookshops.

Read the chapter indicated, or part of the chapter, with a loud voice if you can, so you get used to hearing your own voice, and then try to answer the following questions:

1. Is there an *example* I must follow?
2. Is there a *command* I must obey?
3. Is there a *promise* I may appropriate in faith?
4. Is there a *warning* I must pay attention to?
5. Is there a particular *sin*, or sinful way, which I must confess and abandon?
6. What does God's Spirit tell me about the Father and the Son?

Of course each of us can extend this list with further questions. (The important thing is, did I understand what I have just read?).

Although I knew that my sins had been forgiven, I was very conscious of being an utter failure. The harder I tried to please the Lord, the less I succeeded, the more I felt myself a miserable slave to hateful habits and sin. I just could not understand this. Was I not a child of God? Why then did I do those things which I really hated?

The Holy Spirit led me at this point to read the Epistle

to the Romans. Yes, I knew about being justified by
faith through God's wonderful grace. But what about
my being 'dead with Christ'? I had been in a continual
fight with my ugly 'self' all the time. I always came out
defeated from this battle-field. Then I read Romans.
Yes, I had been discovering all right that 'in me, (that is
in my flesh), dwelleth no good thing' (v.18). I hated that
part of me. Then, one night in my bedroom, reading
chapter seven on my knees, I just cried out: 'O, wretched
man that I am, who shall deliver me from the body of this
death?' (v.24). Then I saw how: 'Now then it is not more
I that do it, but sin that dwelleth in me' (v.17). This 'I',
called the 'old man', or 'the body of sin' (Rom 6:6) *had*
been crucified with Christ on the cross two thousand
years ago, God told me! 'I', my 'old self' was now 'dead
to sin' (Rom 6:11), the 'sin that dwells in me'. But sin
that dwells in my nature is not dead; however I am dead
to sin, through having accepted by faith that I died in
Christ, when He died.

Three things became clear to me now: and these are
contained in three key-words in Romans 6.

First: '*Knowing*' (v.6). 'Knowing this, that our old
man is crucified with him, that the body of sin might be
destroyed that henceforth we should not serve sin'.

Second: '*Reckon*' (v.11). 'Likewise reckon ye also
yourselves to be dead indeed unto sin, but alive unto
God through Jesus Christ our Lord'.

Third: '*Yield*' (v.13). 'Neither yield ye your members
as instruments of unrighteousness unto sin: but yield
yourselves unto God (Rom 12:1,2) as those that are alive
from the dead, and your members as instruments of
righteousness unto God'.

In these three words I discovered the secret of victory
over sin, the sin that dwells in me, the old man, my old
nature: *Knowing*, *Reckoning*, *Yielding*!

When the Holy Spirit brings the reality of these three
words to our hearts and consciences we must act upon

this revelation and make a *complete surrender* to the Lord Jesus Christ. It can therefore be seen both as a once for all experience; the climax of a crisis, the moment when we for the first time utterly capitulate to Christ, and as a consequent *daily attitude* of yielding ourselves to Him, of presenting our spirit, and soul and body daily to Him as a living sacrifice, to do with as He pleases.

That particular evening when these truths were brought home to my heart, I did not come to Christ in order to receive forgiveness, for my sins had been forgiven, but that through that same faith through which I received forgiveness I might now also receive deliverance from the power of indwelling sin. As the Holy Spirit would from now on fill me, He would give power greater than the power of sin: 'For the law of the Spirit of life in Christ Jesus hath made me free from the law of sin and death' (Rom 8:2). Hallelujah! I had to learn that either Christ is Lord of all, or He is not Lord at all. We must all be willing to accept the Lordship of Christ in our lives and to be willing to be emptied of self, so that the life of Christ may be manifested through us.

I had now realised what this call to discipleship really meant (Matt 11:29,30). Now 2 Corinthians 5:15 began to take on a new meaning: '...that they which live should not henceforth live unto themselves, but unto him which died for them, and rose again'. A great desire now began to fill my heart to preach the Gospel of Christ to those who had never yet heard it. The first step in that direction was distributing tracts in the streets and pubs of my home-town, and to join with our youth group in open-air evangelism. A friend gave me some literature about missionary work abroad. The articles and photographs in this magazine about the millions who had never yet heard the Gospel moved me to the depth of my heart with pity and compassion and filled me with a deep longing to go and tell them the Gospel.

Someone had once said: 'No one has the right to hear

the Gospel twice before everyone has heard it once'. I shall never forget that night when in a meeting a sister sang:

> So send I you by grace made strong to triumph,
> O'er hosts of hell, o'er darkness, death and sin,
> My name to bear, and in that name to conquer,
> So send I you, My victory to win.
>
> So send I you to take to souls in bondage,
> The word of truth that sets the captive free,
> To break the bonds of sin, to loose death's fetters
> So send I you, to bring the lost to Me.
>
> So send I you My strength to know in weakness,
> My joy in grief, My perfect peace in pain,
> To prove My power, My grace, My promised presence
> So send I you, eternal fruit to gain.
>
> So send I you to bear My cross with patience,
> And then one day with joy to lay it down,
> To hear My voice: 'Well done My faithful servant –
> Come, share My throne, My kingdom and My crown.[1]

'As my Father hath sent me, so send I you'.

Who of us, brother, sister, can remain indifferent to the appeal of these searching words? Can we, dare we not respond? When I arrived home after the meeting where this sister had sung the above hymn, I went to my bedroom and knelt down and said to the Lord: 'Lord Jesus, here am I, send me'.

Soon afterwards I asked to have a talk with two brothers in Christ from my home assembly at the Hague. One of them taught in the youth Bible-class, the other was a close friend of my father's. Both elders had a heart for the Gospel and a real love for souls. They listened graciously as I poured out my heart to them about my

---

[1] So send I you – John W. Peterson. Based on John 20:21. E. Margaret Clarkson, © copyright 1954, 1963 by Singspiration Inc.

exercises and advised me to continue to seek the Lord's guidance. I believe it is right that young people with this sort of exercise should be encouraged to seek the advice of their elder brethren. This is perhaps too often forgotten or ignored and the result may be that one continues to act in an attitude of independence from one's fellow believers. This in fact would be a denial of the principle of the unity of the Body of Christ and brotherly love. It is indeed a great blessing and encouragement for young people when they can actually confide in brethren with more experience who have a real love for them and a comprehension of young people and their exercises. How we need such wise elders!

At this point my reader may well ask the question: 'But how can you be sure of God's guidance in such cases?' God has a purpose with our lives. His will is that we shall know His will and also submit to His guidance in our daily lives. One of the basic conditions to the learning of His will is to recognise and submit to His Lordship in our lives. Romans 12:2 tells us how we shall then be able to discern His will. I pass on a few guide-lines which I have personally found helpful:

1. Be prepared to give unquestioning obedience to God's will.
2. Seek God's will deliberately in your daily Bible reading.
3. Pray for discernment to recognise God's will in your daily circumstances.
4. Be sure that your motives are pure as you seek His will. Will He be glorified?
5. Do that of which you are sure that it is the right thing to do. God has given us sanctified common sense, and God's Spirit daily renews our mind. He puts the desire in our hearts to want only God's will.
6. Use what God has already given or shown you (2 Kings 4:2).

7. Do not act before you are quite sure and have perfect peace.
8. Seek the advice of spiritual believers. (Prov 11:14).
9. Notice doors that open up and doors that close (1 Cor 16:9). Do not be discouraged when the first or second door closes in your face. See how the apostle Paul reacts in Acts 16:6,7,10.
10. Do not go forward unless you are quite sure that you are acting according to the spiritual principles of the Bible.
11. Be flexible about decisions you have taken in the past. Do not think that because God once gave you direction in a certain way that you must now never accept a change of direction. Remember there is God's permissive will and His ultimate will. Even if we make mistakes (and who does not?) we know that God in His tender mercy will overrule. Often God allows many imperfections and shortcomings in our lives because of our human frailty, and sometimes He has to take us in a round-about way in order to get us where He wants us.

We all have so much to learn, especially when we are still young, in order that we may be able to discern the Lord's will. I have experienced this myself also. In my youth the Lord allowed me to come in contact with believers who were a real blessing to me and who have helped me with their advice. I am grateful for them all. But in the end you and I are personally responsible for our actions. I met with a representative of the Worldwide Evangelisation Crusade at the Hague when I was about 19 years old. He told me that service for the Lord in one's own country had a vastly different character from missionary service in so-called primitive or under-developed countries. One would need to have different qualifications and preparation for pioneer missionary service overseas in order to cope with the climate, food, customs, language, peoples' religions, traditions etc. This will be dealt with more specifically at a later stage in this book.

Is Jesus Lord of our emotions (Genesis 12:4,5)

'So Abram departed....(v.4).

We shall never grow in our spiritual life if we refuse to submit to God's will and yield Him unquestioning obedience in our daily lives. Unless we are prepared to give Him the first place in everything, and surrender to Him our spirit, soul and body as a living sacrifice, we shall never learn to know His will. The Lord Jesus wants to reveal His will to us in every situation. For those who have accepted Jesus Christ as LORD, one of the most important things is to know for sure whether one must remain single or marry. Is marriage for you and me? Whom does the Lord want me to marry? God alone knows the future and how best we can serve Him: single or married, with one or two or more children, or no children at all.

Abram had shown his acceptance of God's will by departing from Haran. That was at least a step in the right direction. But it was not yet complete obedience. He still took his relative Lot with him. This Lot was to cause him a very great deal of trouble and heart-ache. One day he would *have* to separate from him. Meanwhile at Haran his father Terah had died. It is very sad that so many believers seem to have to pass through very deep and sorrowful experiences before they are prepared to accept God's will for their lives unreservedly.

The true disciple of Christ must be willing, if asked, to sacrifice the natural in order that he may gain the spiritual. Sometimes natural relationships must, as it were, 'pass through death and resurrection' in order that we may learn that Jesus Christ must come first. (see Phil 3).

Once during my student days at College I thought I had fallen in love with a French girl. I could not concentrate any more on my studies, nor pray in peace. My friend and I had the habit of praying each morning together. We would share our burdens and would pray for each other. One morning I shared my burden about this French girl with my friend, who, when he had heard my story suddenly burst out laughing. 'Cor, chum,' he said, 'this is funny; I am just as upset over the same girl as you!' I must confess that I was quite annoyed with myself for having been such an easy prey. I told the Lord about it and recognised it for what it was: a momentary deviation and not God's will for me at that time, and peace returned to my heart and mind.

But there is however the danger of 'swinging the pendulum' in a case like this. We become fanatics and conclude that 'marriage is not for me'. But let us remember that we do not ultimately determine this, the Lord does. It sounds of course quite heroic, and some may think it sounds spiritual, when we say that after all marriage is second best, it is unspiritual and a trap of the devil to make us deviate from following and serving Christ. Let us all be quite sure that the enemy of our souls wants to make us unhappy, and he does not care how that happens. Some may have refused marriage who really had no special gift to remain single (see 1 Cor 7:7). Others have rushed into marriage prematurely and finish up going around with a guilt-complex. To others again Satan would suggest that marrying is definitely an unspiritual thing to do. I am afraid that I fell for this plausible argument. I determined not to give this subject any more thought.

Three years later in London I met Audrey (who became my wife and with whom I have been married for more than twenty-five happy years.). This is not the place to tell you how we got married, or how the Lord changed my mind. It was 4 years after our first meeting that we were married. During those four years we had to learn that our quite natural and legitimate affection for each other had nevertheless to be laid on the altar and presented as a sacrifice to Him. Our relationship had to go through the purifying process of death and resurrection. Through this painful process the Lord showed us that He had purposed us for each other and that we had His approval.

There is a sense in which we can hold on to things and persons in a selfish way. We have to be taught how to hold them in fellowship *with* Him (Rom 8:32). Every one of us has to face this question before the Lord: 'Who comes first in my affections? My girl-friend, my boy-friend, my fiancé, my wife, my husband, my mother, my father, my child, my career, hobby, possessions?' We have to learn to say with the apostle Paul: '...what things were gain to me, those I counted loss for Christ' (Phil 3:7). We have to learn to become detached from things and persons in the fellowship of Christ.

Many believers are only ready to let go when they are on their death-bed. But what a priceless privilege and mercy of the Lord when the love of Christ, and our love for Him, constrains us to accept these terms, so that in all things He might have the pre-eminence. Until we have clearly decided once for always that Jesus Christ must come first in our lives, we ought not to contemplate any service for Him either at home or abroad.

The Holy Spirit often reminded us of this lesson during our first ten years in the Middle East. We were then in Egypt. Soon after our arrival the Suez-canal crisis developed and danger threatened us. This was followed by a long and uncertain period during the regime of Gamal Abd el Nasser. We often felt that although 'today' we might still be in Egypt, it was quite possible that 'tomorrow' we might have to leave suddenly and leave all behind. It certainly helped us not to become too attached to things. We often used to look at our few possessions in that small Egyptian village and say to each other 'let us not get too attached to this and that then we will not find it too hard when we have to leave it all.' But it was not easy when it came.

Later at the end of another ten years in the Lebanon we had this very same lesson brought home to our hearts. We suddenly had to flee that poor country, wrecked by civil war, and leave everything behind. We arrived at London airport with our six smaller children with a few suitcases of clothes. If we can really let go the things of this earth, or at least not cleave to them, we would spare ourselves a lot of grief in case one day we had to abandon them all. How often we have to confess with the Psalmist: 'My soul cleaveth unto the dust...' (Ps 119:25). And then, we are so very conscious of our own rights, position, and personal honour, that we find it often terribly difficult not to insist on these rights but let them go.

Giving up our personal rights (Genesis 13:5)

Those servants of Abram and Lot could not get on together. There was often strife and hard words between them. Very strong differences of opinion! Each one of them insisting upon his own rights. This often happens unfortunately, even between believers, and especially with strong and forceful personalities. Does it ever happen to you? We are so sure that we are right and the other is wrong. How much of God's work is ruined because of clashes of personalities. In the family, at work, in the Assembly, in service for the Lord at home, as well as on the mission-field, believers fall out with each other.

If we cannot get along with people where we are right now at this moment, with our parents, brothers and sisters, the boss and our colleagues at work, a change of place or country will not change our personality. Only the cross of Christ can change our personality. But we reason as follows: 'If only my father and mother would change their attitude, or that awful child, that selfish brother or sister, that "impossible" person!' But apparently it never seems to dawn on us that *we* might have to change.

Well, Abram did have legitimate rights, did he not? He *was* Lot's uncle after all. He was therefore entitled to respect and priority in choosing which way he would go. But what does Abram do? He refuses to insist on his own rightful place of priority and allows Lot to make the first choice. It seems that Abram is going to lose heavily by letting Lot be 'selfish'. But this is, of course, pure human reasoning. He who lets God choose for him will always gain spiritually. In all this we see Abram's amazing humility.

Humility is the willingness not to insist on my own rights, opinions, convictions and interpretations. Humility is the very foundation on which service for Christ must be done. Unless we understand this we will cause untold trouble wherever we try to serve the Lord, whether at home or on the foreign fields of service.

When I arrived in Egypt for the first time as a young man of 25 years, I quickly saw that there were a lot of 'wrong' practices, according to my point of view, in the local circle of believers in Tema, Upper Egypt. I was really convinced that those dear believers needed a lot of correction and that I ought to put them right.

Be careful, my friend, whoever you are, who arrives in a new situation, perhaps in your own country, or on the mission-field, with your pre-conceived ideas of what is right and what is wrong. You may cause a lot of harm to your fellow-missionaries and your national brothers and sisters in Christ by insisting that your opinion is the right one.

When I began to pray to the Lord to help me put these matters right, the Lord asked me: 'Why do you think these things are wrong? Is it because you were brought up amongst the believers in Holland? Is it perhaps only a matter of opinion, or a certain interpretation, or is it a matter of doctrinal and fundamental importance?' I must confess that in most cases, it was purely a matter of opinion.

The apostle Paul thought it necessary, and was no doubt led by the Holy Spirit, to devote about four whole chapters in his Epistles on the theme: 'When Christians differ, what then?' How must Christians solve their problems of differences in interpretation between themselves? Let us not forget that we may win an argument but lose a brother believer, or a seeking soul.

In the Epistle to the Romans 14:1 – 15:7, we find three interesting expressions which may help us in determining what our attitude should be in a difference of opinion. When we do not have a chapter or a verse in scripture which prescribes what our attitude should be, let us not be dogmatic and insist on the absolute correctness of our own interpretation.

The first expression is found in 14:1–12 (and especially 15:7): RECEIVE YE ONE ANOTHER. Receive one another as children of God, having the same life in Christ, possessing the same Holy Spirit. Receive one another 'as Christ also received us to the glory of God'.

The second expression is found in 14:13–33, and especially in 19: EDIFY ONE ANOTHER.

The last expression is found in 15:1–7 and especially in 2: PLEASE YOUR NEIGHBOUR. This of course does not mean that one must 'be nice' to him even when he is on a wrong path, because Paul immediately adds what should be the aim of our pleasing him: 'for his good to edification.'

Let us repeat again that especially those who serve the Lord, or desire to serve Him on the foreign fields, must take this lesson to heart BEFORE ever they set foot on foreign soil. Let us remember: wherever you go, you go there as a *servant*, not as a *lord*. You will most probably see things amongst Christians in other lands which may surprise you, and which you do not want to do yourself.

But then ask yourself this question: 'Is it wrong because scripture tells me, or is it only a matter of personal opinion?' Perhaps those believers would be shocked to see the things you allow in your own 'home-situation'.

Unworthy motives: refusing the world's favours
(Genesis 14:21–23)

The Holy Spirit will examine every motive of our hearts. Why do we want to do a certain thing? Why do you feel that you must serve the Lord? Is it perhaps so that people will then say about you: 'Oh, is not that a wonderfully spiritual person!'? Perhaps it is so that we might feel rather superior towards those of our brothers and sisters in Christ who are not in 'full time' service for Christ.

Some may feel that they could serve the Lord much better if only they could quit their job (1 Cor 7:17–23) – but the real reason may be that they are bored with the daily 'hum-drum' of doing the same work all the time. They are really looking for some excitement, for a change. Perhaps they cannot get on very well with the manager at work, or their colleagues, or maybe the salary they earn is too low, or there is no hope of promotion anyway in the future! Such motives are of course totally unworthy and the Holy Spirit would never support or tolerate any such motives. In fact, if any one dares to serve the Lord from any motive other than to do God's will, his service will be fruitless, powerless, and will lack the Lord's approval.

How then can we be sure of God's will in this matter? Abram will again be our example. Abram had just gained a tremendous victory over five hostile kings. You know perhaps from your own experience how you feel 'good' after a spiritual victory. Now is the time to watch out. It takes a spiritual believer to remain humble and dependent upon the Lord after such a victory.

Satan opposes the believer either as a 'roaring lion' (think of those five enemy-kings), or as an 'angel of light' (think of the king of Sodom). When the enemy comes as a roaring lion we can at least recognize him for what he is. But when he comes to us as an angel of light, we really need 'to be strengthened with might by his Spirit in the inner man' (see Eph 3:16).

God saw Abram's need at this moment and therefore sent to him Melchizedek, who offered him bread and wine. It was through this communion of bread and wine in company with Melchizedek that Abram seemed to receive that necessary spiritual discernment in order to face a much more subtle temptation which came to him presently by way of the 'generous' offer of the king of Sodom. Abram was able to refuse this 'favour' because he had his eyes on the Lord and would not rob God of His glory.

Our hearts are deceitful above all things, and desperately wicked: who can know it? (says Jer 17:9). Who does not have a struggle when the world offers her 'favours' for a work done perhaps for the Lord? Are we strong enough at such a time and spiritual enough to refuse? Do we think that God ignores the fact that any one of His servants, by accepting worldly favour, would give thereby the world the opportunity to say: 'We have enriched him, we have honoured him'?

It should be clear to us all that servants of God who accept worldly favours for work done for Him, will suffer loss at the judgment seat of Christ (Matt 6:2,5,16). But let us not look around us at what other servants may do and allow. Let us rather examine ourselves. If we should find any unworthy motives in our hearts in relation to the service of the Lord are we willing right now to judge them and put them away?

Impatience is sin (Genesis 17:15–22)

One of the most difficult lessons to learn in the school of God is: to have patience. (Heb 10:36; 2 Pet 1:6). It seems that we poor human beings can only learn this through suffering. How many and varied are these sufferings which we may inflict upon ourselves through our own impatience and lack of true submission to the will of God. It may be that we suffer *because* we walk in God's will. But it is also possible that we suffer because we are out of harmony with the Lord. And God just seems to allow it all.

It is not wrong for a believer to ask an anguished and honest: 'Why God?'. Of course, it does depend whether the attitude in which we ask this question is one of rebellion. Then it is wrong and we will receive no reply. But if it is with a broken spirit and a contrite heart and a spirit of submission, then God will teach us to have confidence in Him and to trust Him. We may not even then get an answer, but He gives us His peace that passes all understanding. 'Now no chastening for the present seemeth to be joyous but grievous; nevertheless afterward it yieldeth the peaceable fruit of righteousness unto them which are exercised thereby" (Heb 12:11).

I remember how once I was passing through a very difficult circumstance and a friend sent me the following lines:

> 'Ill that He blesses is most good,
> And unblest "good" is ill;
> And all is right that seems most wrong
> If it be His blest will'
> *Author unknown*

There are believers who are absolutely convinced that they must serve the Lord 'somewhere else', but definitely not 'at home' with that helpless and dependent parent, that difficult child...but abroad somewhere on the mission field. Once a lady came to Mr Spurgeon saying she felt sure she was called to the mission field. Mr Spurgeon asked her whether she had any responsibilities. 'Oh, yes' she said, 'I am mother of ten children'. 'Well, Madam,' said Mr Spurgeon, 'God certainly provided you with a mission field on your doorstep in your own home.'

For some of us service for Christ means that He has called us to live for Him just where we are right now: with that bed-ridden person, that member of the family, that unfortunate child, in that impossible situation, somewhere as it were 'behind the scenes' unnoticed. Others think that God is making a big mistake when He gives them a task to do for Him which is not in the limelight; an uninteresting and unrewarding task. Is that how you feel?

No doubt Abram's patience with God was running out. He did not agree with God's way of doing things. This had now been going on for years, and still no change. God must have forgotten, or He did not care any more. The time had come, so said Abram, that he should 'help' God a little. Does not the proverb say: 'God helps those who help themselves'? Well then! The circumstances seemed so favourable and indicated no doubt that he was doing the right thing. Did not even his wife encourage him in it? It must be right.

This is probably what Jonah the prophet also thought when he saw that all his circumstances were 'in his favour'. Just think of that ship there in the harbour of Joppa: it was just waiting there to take him where he wanted to go. And imagine the providence that had supplied him with just enough money to cover the fare. Everything 'down' to Joppa had been so wonderfully smooth. Too smooth! When we want to do our own will we can always manage to interpret our circumstances as being favourable.

But impatience is really self-will unrestrained. We are

impatient with those at home. If only we could change them, or that they would simply change! We try our best to change them, but we never for one moment consider whether it is perhaps ourselves that ought to change. And so we are impatient with our fellow-believers. We just cannot understand why they are so blind as not to see that we are really called to serve the Lord. Well, we decide to go ahead anyway with our plans, with or without their approval. Instead of trying to accept the situation as from the Lord and so have peace, and give the Lord time to make things clearer for ourselves as well as for our brethren, we force our way through to get what we want, in spite of all the heart-ache and sorrow we may thereby cause others.

Patience is one of the most important requirements in our contacts with others, whether at home or abroad, whether at work or in our place of worship. We shall never be a blessing unless we learn to be patient and have patience with those with whom we come in contact.

Those who contemplate serving the Lord in primitive conditions, so much unlike 'home', will realise the great need for patience even more. Everything is going to be a lot different from what you have been accustomed to and often taken for granted. There are the problems of climate and customs, peoples and languages, food and drink etc. Patience will be sorely tried. Just the fact that one may have to learn one or two foreign languages will require much patience and persistence.

If you find it difficult now to accept correction from others you had better not contemplate service abroad. In learning a new and difficult language, one of course makes stupid mistakes. But never forget that you will learn best from your mistakes — if they are corrected! Like that missionary friend of ours in Upper Egypt who taught a group of girls. She had to discipline one of them and said to her in Arabic: 'Go, stand in that corner' (at least that is what she *thought* she had said!). All the girls started to giggle and laugh. What our friend had actually said was: 'Kiss that wall'! It was only a very small mistake of a wrong emphasis but it changed the whole meaning and had the opposite effect to what she wanted. If it is already quite humiliating as an adult to be corrected all the time by other adults, how mortifying it can be when one is corrected by a child noticing our funny mistakes.

In lands with tropical climates people are generally more deliberate and slow in their actions; they do not rush around as madly as people in colder climates. We have to accept that when living among them. This will be a great trial for a restless and energetic soul. But we must learn to 'sit where they sit' if we really want to be of service to them and win their confidence. Often one may have to eat and sleep and live in extremely primitive circumstances with dust and dirt, fleas and flies, mosquitoes and mud, scorpions, serpents and spiders.

I remember a little incident in Tema (Upper Egyptian village). We had a very old army Jeep, probably a left over from the battle of El Alamein during the second world war. The country roads in Upper Egypt were all extremely dusty because it hardly ever rains and it is mostly sunny all the year round. It is better therefore for your car to have a colour that will not show up the dust too much: grey for instance. So I went one day to our village painter and asked him to spray my Jeep grey. 'Right you are, sir. Come back tomorrow and it will be ready', he said. The next day as I approached the painter's workshop, I saw in the distance that our Jeep had indeed an entirely 'new look'. The man had painted it a gleaming heavenly blue. I asked him why in the world he had sprayed it that colour. 'Oh, I like this colour much better. Don't you, Mr. Bruins?' was his simple answer. I needed much self-control and patience at that moment.

And then having to put up with all sorts of cheating: ground rice mixed up with your sugar, live pigeons you buy in the market stuffed so full with corn that they weigh heavier, meat you buy in the street, covered with flies, and having been injected with lots of water to make it heavier and therefore more expensive, and of course milk thinned with water, and always having to bargain in order not to be cheated too much! Yet all these little incidents and irritations are to teach us patience and submission to His will in the smallest details of our daily life.

Suppose now that God has planned that you and I shall serve Him 'at home', would we be willing to accept it? If God wants you to look after that sick, old and invalid relative, will you accept that? If God has planned a humble service for you right where you are, will you accept it and not impatiently try to serve Him somewhere else?

God rejected Abram's proposition: 'O that Ishmael might live before thee' (Gen 17·18). God will always refuse what is of our old nature. God showed him again what His will was for Abram. But Abram having taken a wrong course must suffer the consequences of his act of impatience. We must learn that God's will must be done where He chooses, and in the way that He reveals, and at the time He will indicate.

The good can be the enemy of the best (Genesis 22)

Abraham had been willing to leave his home, his parents, his relatives, his country, and to walk by faith depending upon God alone. Was not this sufficient? Abraham had become the 'friend of God'. God had blessed him richly in spiritual as well as material things. He had made mistakes, but had confessed them, and God had forgiven him and restored him. He had become a man with a very rich experience and was now over 100 years old. He had believed God's word of promise, and God had declared that Abraham had been accepted by Him (declared righteous) because of his faith in Him. And so God had at last given him that son for whom he had longed so much and prayed so fervently many long years.

His son Isaac! Yes, Abraham's heart was filled with gratitude towards God when he thought of his son Isaac. In that boy were all his hopes for the future. His heart was knit to the heart of Isaac; they loved each other so much. How wonderful this relationship was between father and son! God had given it, God was in it, God approved of it, and it was all in the will of God for Abraham. His cup ran over! And then the unbelievable happened! The impossible! It was such a paradox! Had Abraham really understood? It was not logical: 'Take now thy son, thine only son Isaac, whom thou lovest, and get thee into the land of Moriah; and offer him there for a burnt offering upon one of the mountains which I will tell thee of' (Gen 22:2).

How can God give something with His right hand, and then take it away again with His left? Only implicit trust in His love and wisdom will help us submit where we cannot understand. It is that same lesson again which Abraham had to learn: 'Who comes first in your life?' We do not fully realise the corrupt selfishness of our own hearts and natures. The more it is revealed to us, the more we cry out with Job: 'I abhor myself, and repent in dust and ashes' (Job 42:6).

Paul writes: 'I am crucified with Christ: nevertheless I live; yet not I...' (Gal 2:20). But to experience the truth of that in reality is not so simple. It is a fact that our 'flesh', that is what we are by nature, which is also called 'the old man' (Rom 6:6), is always ready as it were to do all possible kinds of religious stunts and apparently honour and serve God, if only it can remain alive! This inwardly corrupt, but outwardly quite religious 'self' is well able to give out tracts, teach in the Sunday school, sing in the choir, speak in the open air, do missionary work, as long as it is not discovered for what it really is, and as long it can escape the verdict of the cross of Christ. They who want to be acceptable to God must be prepared to be identified with Christ's death.

Paul says that if a man were able to speak all human languages and even speak like an angel, and prophesy, and know all mysteries, and have miracle-working faith that could move mountains and raise the dead, but did not have love, it would all be worthless. A man might offer up all his possessions, and, driven by a sense of the heroic, even die by letting himself be burned. But it would all be worthless before God, and unacceptable to Him if the motive that constrained him was not love.

Strange and paradoxical as it might seem: there is latent in all our hearts what I would call 'the sense of the heroic'. It is similar in principle to what men today call masochism: a spiritual kind of masochism, by which I mean a perversion from which the sufferer derives 'pleasure' from self inflicted pain and humiliation.

We can be secretly proud of our 'humility'. I have known cases where earnest believers stood up in front of others, or in the midst of a group, to lay bare their innermost being, telling of all the ugliness and corruption they were conscious of, confessing it publicly in detail. Thereby, perhaps unconsciously to themselves, they were defiling those who listened to them. The effect they hoped to produce was perhaps that they would be seen as so terribly honest and humble to be even willing to let others see how bad they were. It was in fact a kind of spiritual exhibitionism. They had made great sacrifices: married couples that had given up their homes and good jobs and position, all for Christ.

Of course all this is admirable, but you do not talk, or brag about it. In Matthew 19:27 we find Peter saying: 'Behold, we have forsaken all, and followed thee; what shall we have therefore?' Did he also think that sacrifice for Christ is a virtue that must be rewarded? Do some of us also crave for recognition of our willingness to sacrifice and feel that we can achieve this by telling others how much we have given up for Him? Sacrifice for Christ then becomes a goal in itself and thereby loses all its value for the Lord. Yes, I must confess that I can find this also in my own heart. Can you find it in yours?

It is not so much what we are prepared to *do* and *sacrifice* for the Lord that counts, but whether God is able to conform us to the image of His blessed Son. What is God able to do with and in you and me? God's ultimate purpose is to conform us to Christ's image (Rom 8:29). Service for Him is only one of the fruits of intimate relationship with Christ. It is never an end in itself. That is why our aim should not be the *service* or the *mission field*! as an end in itself. Because if that particular mission field or that particular service which we felt called to, becomes an unobtainable goal, then at least we have not lost the purpose for our existence. For that purpose is nothing less than attachment to Jesus Christ, following Him wherever He leads.

Looking back over our own lives my wife and I can also detect periods in which we have had to learn this most important lesson. God had graciously permitted that in my youth I had become an accepted candidate of a worldwide missionary society for overseas missionary work. I had five years' preparation through Bible-school, a medical school, a French language school and a period of 9 months as a probationary prior to my being accepted by the mission board at head-quarters.

Meanwhile Audrey and I had met in London. We were both absolutely sure that God meant us for each other. But then a member of the mission board told me that the other members could not accept me as a candidate so long as I had not broken off my relationship with Audrey. These were the rules of the board. The reasons given were these: Audrey would have to follow a missionary preparation of 2 – 3 years, after she had finished her nursing training, and a further year at least at the language school in Paris. All this would take some 4 – 5 years before we could even think of marriage. I was told that this relationship would only hinder my future service for Christ on the mission field.

But how could this be possible? Had not God called us both and given us to each other so that we might serve Him together? Did the Lord Jesus not send His disciples two by two? It all seemed a paradox similar to Abraham's situation. After much heart-searching we felt that nevertheless, if this was God's will for us both *at this stage*, we must accept it and submit to it, and give each other back to Him. We did so but were nevertheless convinced that we were destined for each other, and that our Lord Jesus would yet bring us together again as it were through death and resurrection. We had to learn that ALL must be laid on the altar, the dearest and the best.

At this time I came across the following poem:

> When God wants to drill a man,
> And thrill a man,
> And skill a man,
> When God wants to mould a man
> To play the noblest part;
> When He yearns with all His heart
> To create so great and bold a man
> That all the world shall be amazed,
> Watch His methods, watch His ways!
> How He ruthlessly perfects
> When He royally elects!
> How He hammers him and hurts him,
> And with mighty blows converts him
> Into trial shapes of clay which
> Only God can understand
> While his tortured heart is crying
> And he lifts beseeching hands!
> How He bends but never breaks
> When His good He undertakes;
> How He uses whom He chooses
> And with every purpose fuses him,

By every act induces him
To try His splendour out –
God knows what He is about!
Author unknown

We all have to learn by experience what the difference is between counting all things loss for Christ, and *suffering* the loss of all things to win Christ' (Phil 3:8). When we *count* a thing loss, it can be simply a mental attitude which we adopt concerning some person or thing. But when we *suffer* the loss of a person or thing, then we actually feel the sword going through our soul; we feel the pain and anguish of it. Blessed is he who can sing with the hymn-writer:

Have Thine own way, Lord,
Have Thine own way;
Hold o'er my being
Absolute sway.
Fill with Thy Spirit
Till all shall see
Christ only, always,
Living in me.
A. A. Pollard, 1862–1934

'And Abraham rose up early in the morning...and went unto the place of which God had told him.' (v.3). Abraham obeyed, without argument. He did not understand 'why', but he knew the loving and merciful and kind heart of his God. That was sufficient for Abraham. Is that also sufficient for you?

5

MOSES – THE MEEKEST SERVANT OF GOD

The man of action (Exodus 2:11)

Moses' intentions were admirable. He did so want to help his brethren. There was so much need around, so much misery and bondage: those poor, poor creatures! Was not he young and strong and full of burning zeal for the name of the Lord his God? He was just overwhelmed with the crying need for helping hands: to do something to change the lot of these poor people. He saw it so clearly: what was required *now*, was action! Of course he must *do* something! He could not remain passive, indifferent and inactive.

But Moses, as well as ourselves, had to learn that the need does not necessarily also constitute the *call*. There is a tremendous spiritual need everywhere in the world today, but if God has not called you or me personally for a specific task He has in mind for us, then what we ought to do is *wait* His time. He will make it clear.

The Lord Jesus had said: 'The harvest truly is great, but the labourers are few: *pray* ye therefore the Lord of the harvest, that he would send forth labourers into his harvest' (Luke 10:2). We therefore start with praying, not with going or doing. Many believers think that the sign of true spirituality is that we do something, we must be active. Otherwise, they think there must be something wrong. But the first thing we have to do when we become aware of the great spiritual need in this world, is to pray that the Lord would send labourers into His harvest.

Then, if the Lord should say to one of us: 'I want to send you', would we be ready to say: 'Here am I. Send me'? Could we be more concerned for the spiritual needs of countless precious souls around us than the Lord Himself? He is the Lord of the harvest, and He alone determines who must do what and where and when and how. Not you, not I. Therefore the most important thing for the spiritual believer to do is to wait prayerfully on the Lord daily for guidance and direction.

Moses acted before God's time had come, and the Lord did not protect him from the consequences of his rash act. The next forty years in the wilderness Moses had to learn his own nothingness and uselessness. Moses thought he was somebody, then forty years later he learned that he was nobody, and the last forty years of his life he experienced that God was *everything*. We must all be emptied of self, then we can be filled with the Holy Spirit and then we shall be ready and open to receive God's mind and will. So Moses felt called to do something. Perhaps you also feel called to do something? How and where must you make a start? It is perhaps useful to say something at this stage about what we could call: 'The Exercise of Gift'.

This is indeed a problem which occupies the minds of many earnest Christians and which is not so easy to answer. We just desire to pass on some thoughts on the subject, but we do so with the consciousness that there are others more qualified than ourselves who are better able to deal with this subject.

The *call* of God is always accompanied by a gift and the ability to execute that call. A call to a specific ministry is a very personal matter: '... the Spirit dividing to every man severally as he will.' (1 Cor 12:11). As a 'member' in the body of Christ every believer has a function to perform (see 1 Cor 12; Rom 12). The call of the Lord to you and me is therefore always related to the function we perform in the body, which is the Church. 'A gift therefore is a gift *in* the body and *for* the body, just as a member in the human body functions on behalf of the whole body. My eye for instance looks on behalf of my whole body, my foot walks for my whole body' (J. N. Darby). This is a very important principle to remember!

The exercise of a call to the service of the Lord is not an isolated matter which only concerns you or me. True, the call is personal, but the exercise of it, and how, and why, and when, is very closely associated with the functions of the other members in the body: my fellow-believers, my brothers and sisters in Christ, and if I am married, my wife. It is therefore quite wrong for anyone to think that he can exercise his ministry independent of the rest of the body. The Spirit of God will never work like that. It would be a direct contradiction of the fact of the unity of the body of Christ.

What could be the cause of a member in our body not functioning properly? Sickness! In the body of Christ (the Church) there must be perfect harmony between all the members in order that all the functions can be properly executed and contribute to the well-being of the whole body. But I as a member might be 'ill' and so cause disharmony. Paul warns about that in Romans 12:3: 'For I say, through the grace given unto me, to every man that is among you, not to think of himself more highly than he ought to think; but to think soberly, according as God hath dealt to every man the measure of faith'. I may imagine for instance that I ought to perform a function to which the Lord has not called me, nor given me any ability. We often see ourselves in quite a different light from what others, our fellow-believers, discern in us.

How does one know that one is called, that one has received a gift and what that particular gift is? No doubt the Holy Spirit will reveal it not only to our own hearts, but to others as well. According to Matthew 25:14–30 we have to *use* our gift, and trade with our talent. *In* the use of it, when we for instance 'show forth the praises of him who hath called us out of darkness into his marvellous light' (1 Pet 2:9), it will become apparent whether we have been gifted of the Lord, and with what gift. With that gift, and in dependence upon the Lord, we shall seek to serve the children of God or preach the Gospel.

But a brother may think he has a gift, and yet he does not edify the saints, and there is apparently no fruit from his labours. What then? This may be an indication that the particular brother is not being led by the Holy Spirit. His brethren will then have to try with much prayer and love and great tact to help this brother. If the brother is not willing to listen to his brethren, then the case becomes more complicated, but it is not our aim here to deal with that.

It is good to remain humble, and not to become angry or irritated when others draw our attention to the fact that we may not be fitted for *that* particular service we are trying to do: '...to every man according to his several ability...'.

Many were born with natural gifts. There are those, for instance, who just love children, whilst others feel more at home with young people. Others again have a very sensitive heart full of sympathy and patience for those who suffer or who are elderly or bed-ridden. There are gifted brothers who administer and organise, and people who have great facility with languages, and who are able to adapt themselves to any and every situation and all sorts of people with great ease.

A believer surrenders his or her total being into the hands of the Lord Jesus, and the Holy Spirit will purify and sanctify these natural gifts and energise them, and through their use in dependence upon the Lord these gifts will develop and increase. But each one should remain within the limits of the gift which he has received. The nose cannot possibly take over the function of the foot, and the eye can never be a substitute for the mouth. Paul, who had more than one gift, was exceptional.

What is demanded of us is that we should be sober and make a realistic appraisal of what we have received, and that we pray for guidance so that we do not cause any difficulties amongst our fellow-believers because of our self-opinionated attitude and independent action. God alone calls us and also determines the moment in which we shall obey that call as well as what that call entails.

Let us remember that there are various aspects to a call:

1. There is first of all the divine aspect: He calls, and He sends forth.

2. Secondly there is the human aspect: this has to do with the members in the body of Christ: the believers.

We see these principles clearly illustrated in Acts 13:

(a) the Holy Spirit *separates* Paul and Barnabas (they had long since obeyed the call, they were already very active teachers and prophets). Besides Paul and Barnabas there were Simeon, Lucius and Manaen at Antioch, all able and gifted, and yet they were not separated or chosen for this special service.

(b) All these brothers were well-known amongst the believers as prophets and teachers. Their gifts were recognised by all. It was therefore not a question of someone recently converted, or a brother who up till this moment had not been actively engaged in any service who suddenly announces to his brethren that he feels definitely 'called' to go out as a missionary.

(c) There is complete harmony at Antioch, and there is full fellowship with Paul and Barnabas. We read in v.3 that the brethren 'let them go' (from the verb '*apoluo*', meaning to release or let go). This is important. The fundamental idea here is not that the brothers, or the assembly at Antioch 'sent them forth': because the Lord alone has that prerogative.

(d) This fellowship and identification of the believers at Antioch with these two brethren is further emphasized in Acts 14:26–28.

In the case of Timothy we see how again these same principles are applied (Acts 16:1–5)

(a) Paul wants to take Timothy with him as his fellow-worker. But Paul recognises what we could call 'the law of the body'. Not that Paul asks for the *approval* or consent of the brothers at Lystra and Iconium. Because God is the Giver of the gift, it is quite sufficient that one has *His* approval. Of course, if the spiritual condition of the other fellow-believers is good (as well as the spiritual condition of him who has received a grace-gift), then there will be harmony.

(b) The brothers of Lystra and Iconium, who all knew Timothy very well, give a good account of him; they recommend him, and identify themselves with him. But let us mark well: this did not mean that Timothy was now appointed by them, or that he needed the approbation or assent of one or more believers, or of the assembly.

Paul himself did not wait for the assent of others (Gal 1:16), and the same was true with Apollos (Acts 18:24–28). Neither does Acts 13 speak of approval of the assembly there at Antioch. Paul and Barnabas had already been several years in the work of the Lord. It is perhaps good to remind ourselves that it was only after he had laboured for 14 years in many places with much blessing that Paul became officially recognised by the apostles, obviously because they all saw that he had been clearly called by God. But Paul never insisted that they should recognise him. Anyone who feels that the Lord has called him or her likewise has no right to insist on recognition by others.

Of course it is God's purpose that a servant should have the confidence of his fellow-believers. But those fellow-believers can only give that confidence when the Lord has shown them personally that the brother concerned has indeed been called to His service. Consequently there will then be no problem whatsoever about the support of that brother with regard to his spiritual as well as his material needs.

But here arises another question: when is it appropriate for anyone, who feels the Lord calling him, to abandon his ordinary earthly service or work? Here follow the words of another servant: 'In the first place he should already be actively engaged in service for the Lord. In other words, he does not enter the Lord's service the moment he decides to give up his ordinary profession, but he takes this decision *because* he *is* already actively engaged in the service of the Lord. Were he not already a servant of the Lord, then he would not have the right to live of the service of the Lord'.

But one of my readers may say: suppose now that personally I find it difficult to accept that brother so-and-so has received a gift and works for the Lord. In this case how do I determine my attitude toward this brother? I believe that the apostle Paul gives us a striking example in Philippians 1:15–18. He says: 'What then? notwithstanding, every way, whether in pretence, or in truth, Christ is preached; and I therein do rejoice, yea, and will rejoice' (further examples are possibly found in Numbers 11:26–29 and Luke 9:49, 50). In any case, one should definitely not oppose, break down, or criticise, but rather continue to pray for the person concerned.

C. H. Mackintosh writes the following:

Undoubtedly we ought to strive by all means for unity in the work, but we should never allow that thereby a rift is caused in the matter of personal work, or to come in between a servant and his Master. We must not attempt to reduce everything to a mere lifeless uniformity, or to limit the different activities in the service of Christ, by seeking to keep them within the old forms which we ourselves have invented! We must strive in all earnestness to combine a hearty unity with the greatest measure of diversity of operations. Both will be promoted in a healthy way if we remember that we are all called to work together under Christ. Here lies the great secret: together under Christ! Let us hold fast what that really means. It will help us to recognise and appreciate the methods and ways of another, even although these may differ from ours. It will also preserve us from thinking too much of our own way of working, for we shall see that we are all but fellow-labourers together in the one great harvest field.

Personally I must confess that I have had to learn all these things the hard way. God in His grace had permitted me to join a missionary society. But my membership raised so many questions in my heart. Amongst other things there were at head-quarters those marvellous and unforgettable prayer meetings going on for hours. What fervour, what zeal and what 'unity'! Yes, we were all united, six days of the week, in our vision of world-evangelisation in our day and generation. Our 'disunity' became so much the more apparent on Sundays when all of us went off each one to his own denomination and church. This seemed to me so contradictory! The emphasis seemed to me to be mainly on what we must do *for* God through evangelisation. The question of what God could do in us, or whether He received the worship due to Him, never seemed to be a priority, but of rather secondary importance.

During my language study in Paris the Spirit of God began to show me the preciousness of the unity of the

Assembly as the body of Christ. There was on the one hand our calling as a *holy* priesthood: going into the presence of the Lord God as worshippers; and on the other hand our calling to a *royal* priesthood: shown in our going forth to announce the praise of him who hath called us out of darkness into his marvellous light (1 Pet 2:5–9). I had never really understood the importance of my calling as a worshipper, I had been so busy up till now going out evangelising.

I began to see now the difference between a human organisation and the living organism which is the Church. It came to me like the force of a revelation. It changed my whole outlook, or rather, it brought many things into a clearer (and in my opinion) more balanced Biblical perspective. My only vision up till now had been world evangelisation. I had not now lost that vision, or the love for souls and the Gospel. But I now saw the possibility of not having to over-emphasize the one truth at the expense of another truth. Worship and evangelism must go inseparably together.

Being faithful to the truth of gathering to the Name of the Lord Jesus Christ only, acknowledging Him alone as the living glorified Head in heaven, in separation from all human systems and sectarian principles, can indeed go hand in hand with a great love for souls and evangelism. Someone has once expressed it as follows: 'The evangelist should be like a compass, with one foot stationary in a scriptural assembly, and with the other foot sweeping the world with the Gospel and bringing converts into the assembly'. Apart from evangelism there would never have been the Church. Neither can the Assembly on earth continue its existence without sustained and intensive evangelistic effort.

Paul was at the same time a minister of the Gospel as well as a minister of the Church (see Col 1:23, 25). He considered his evangelistic ministry as directly linked with priestly service (see Rom 15:16). We repeat, the priestly element (entering into the sanctuary to worship in Spirit and in truth, Jn 4:24 and 1 Pet 2:5), and the levitical element (the going out and forth to show the praises of our Lord, 1 Pet 2:9), were in Paul's view united. What therefore God has joined together, let no man separate! Within the framework of the local representation of the universal Church of Christ, the gifts which Christ has given as we find them enumerated in Ephesians 4:11 can be developed and should be encouraged.

At this stage I began to ask myself the question: 'Why then was I a member of an organisation? Was I not in fact a living member in a living organism (the Church) and livingly and organically linked with other members? And if I sought to be faithful to the principles of the New Testament Church and gather together with true believers on the only true and scriptural basis of the unity of the body of Christ, how then could I remain in a human organisation? To evangelise or minister the Word of God without the continuous prayer-fellowship of those with whom I also worshipped together and walked the same way together was unthinkable. To go off on my own and seek to serve the Lord in independence of my brothers and sisters in Christ? In this way not to have to submit to godly discipline? To follow my own thoughts and will and to bear not correction? This surely was not the Lord's way for me.

How well I remember that afternoon at the home of brother Lemkes! Four or five other brothers were also present. They had invited me to come and talk with them. They wanted to know why I was so sure that the Lord wanted me to go to Egypt. It was a long and wonderful story I was able to tell that afternoon of the way in which the Lord had led me these past five years. The brothers showed much understanding and feeling for what they heard, but they could only – and quite rightly so – say that they would all pray the Lord to give them wisdom and guidance in order to be able to advise me and give me their opinion. Their advice was that I should give up my connection with the missionary organisation, and for the time being engage myself in my original profession as book-keeper in order to earn my living. They would let me know the moment the Lord had made things clear to them.

And so it was that I found myself behind a typewriter in the office of brother van den Bosch! What had I done? Was this indeed God's will for me? How could I possibly have returned to that from which the Lord had called me away five years ago to serve Him? Had not God called me then? Was it not my duty and responsibility to go and tell poor sinners everywhere of His wonderful love? But here, in this office everything seemed to have come to an end. God put my tears which I wept during those months in His bottle (Ps 56:8) – tears of burning desire and love for Him and lost men and women, and tears of disappointment at having arrived seemingly at a dead end in the road.

But then I heard His gentle voice: 'Cor, you have showed that you were willing to leave your father and your mother, your country, in order to follow Me. Yes, you have also been willing to lay Audrey as a sacrifice upon the altar. But there is still something else that you must offer up as a sacrifice upon the altar, and that is your *call*. If I should ask you to give up this desire to serve on the mission field; if I should tell you that I do not want you to serve Me, and that your mouth must remain closed for always, because I wanted that – would you be willing to obey and follow Me there also? Nobody knows the battle I fought, nobody knows but Jesus. He showed me that in order to win Him *everything else* must be counted loss. This was indeed the end of everything.

My dear reader, have you ever arrived at this point in your experience? This is where God commences with us. Moses too had to learn this through many disappoint-

ments and disillusionments. You and I also must learn
that we are nothing.

The disappointment (Exodus 2:14)

Moses had to flee from the land of Egypt. It is quite
remarkable that we do not read about this in Hebrews
11:24–26. What we read there is in connection with
Moses' inner spiritual attitude, as a man of faith.
'Esteeming the reproach of Christ greater riches than
the treasures in Egypt...by faith he forsook Egypt, *not
fearing* the wrath of the king for he endured, as seeing
him who is invisible.'

Such a man is able to accept the deepest disappointments out of God's hand. He did not look to man; he
only regarded the Lord and what He wanted. In his heart
he had made the decision and given up Egypt: yes, by
faith he had forsaken Egypt. He realised that he must
now follow the Lord at all cost, even if his own brothers
should reject him or misunderstand, misjudge or disap-
point him. How admirably Moses adapted himself to his
new situation. He loved the Lord, and he loved his
brethren who were in such dire need. He had gone out
with the best intentions that day when he killed that
Egyptian. But he did not realise that, mixed up with that
burning zeal, there was much too much of Moses' self.
That had to be purged out on the threshing-floor of the
Lord of the harvest.

A believer may be very sincere, and yet sincerely
wrong, in the way in which he interprets God's will.
Ignorance with regard to God's will and mind and ways
is only considered sinful when a person stubbornly
refuses to accept any correction or advice from others,
or from God Himself. Are we prepared to learn from
our mistakes? Are we willing to accept that our disappointments are God's appointments? God may use
another believer to help me and you. Are we prepared to

accept that help offered as if it were from the Lord Himself? The only way to grow spiritually and in the understanding of God's will is to submit ourselves to the Word of God.

Total submission (Exodus 2:16–22)

Moses learned quickly. He did not sit down and sulk or wallow in self-pity because his brothers had not accepted him or understood his good intentions. He did not become angry with them or lose his temper. He did not say: 'O well, I do not need you anyway; I will get on by myself'. He did not act hurt, as if to say: 'How dare you treat me like that?' He did not act resentfully against the Lord saying: 'If you do not want to use me – well, then I will not do a thing for anybody'. On the contrary, Moses submitted to God's permissive will. He accepted his circumstancs from the hand of the Lord. He was enabled to rise above his own feelings and ask himself what he could still do for others at that moment. He did the obvious things at hand, and helped the daughters of Jethro water their flock (v.17).

There is nothing which more obviously shows that we have a divine mission than the calm and ready manner in which we perform this mission with devotion, whether the circumstances are favourable or not. This ability to accept disappointment and apparent failure quietly and submissively is one of the most necessary requirements for those who desire to serve the Lord – to be able to persevere and stick at the job we are doing although we have no apparent 'success'. It is good to realise that the servant is not called in the first place to be successful, but he is called to be *faithful*.

God allows disappointments; He actually uses them for His own purposes, and overrules them. Paul tells us: 'And we know that all things work together for good to them that love God, to them who are the called according to his purpose.' (Rom 8:28). Are you disappointed? Has the 'door' been slammed shut in your face? Have you failed to reach the goal you had set up for yourself? Do you feel that your fellow-believers, your brothers and sisters in Christ have misjudged you? Hand it all over to the Lord. He has permitted this to happen to you. Go on with Him, and trust Him to bring things to pass. Wait prayerfully and patiently for the Lord to guide you; He will then show you the next step.

Watchfulness (Exodus 3:3)

Forty long years had now passed. Any hope that he might still serve the Lord by going to help his brethren in Egypt had by now been practically extinguished. But Moses faithfully performed his daily work as a shepherd in the wilderness. True submissiveness to the will of God will be manifested by the way in which we perform our daily duties faithfully, patiently and with entire devotion. 'And whatsoever ye do, do it heartily, as to the Lord, and not unto men.' (Col 3:23).

Further it is also very important that we keep our eyes open all the time to discern the way in which God leads and guides and acts. The communion between God and Moses had continued without interruption no doubt. But Moses was most probably not conscious at all of the fact that in the quietness of the wilderness God was preparing him for the greatest task of his life. 'He that is faithful in that which is least is faithful also in much.' (Luke 16:10).

Do you feel that nothing is happening in your life? Do you think your best time is past, that you have lost the best opportunities, that your life is wasted? Never forget that in the life of a believer nothing is considered 'lost' – even disappointments, set-backs and failures should never be considered as lost time. Here is a wonderful word of comfort: 'And I will restore to you the years that

the locust hath eaten, the cankerworm, and the cater-
pillar, and the palmerworm.' (Joel 2:25). Let us be
watchful then, and alert, for then we shall be able to
discern the hand of God in our every day circumstances,
and He will lead us on.

Humility (Exodus 3:11)

'Who am I?' is what we hear Moses say. He has had a
great deal of experience during the forty years in the
wilderness. The Holy Spirit gives a wonderful testimony
of Moses when He says of him: 'Now the man Moses was
very meek, above all the men which were upon the face
of the earth' (Num 12:3). But Moses found himself
totally unsuitable and utterly inadequate to do this impossible thing God was now asking of him. But God
knew Moses better than he knew himself, and God had
been fitting out His servant so that he might act on His
behalf. In the same way as the apostle Paul later, so
Moses had to learn: 'for when I am weak, then am I
strong.' (2 Cor 12:10); and 'that the excellency of the
power may be of God, and not of us.' (2 Cor 4:7).

We all have to learn the same lesson: that we are
nothing, and can do nothing, but that all things are
possible with God. (Mark 10:27). This text from Mark's
Gospel was stuck to the large mirror in our dining room
at home. Every time you looked in this mirror, hung
over the fireplace, these words stared you in the face.
ALL THINGS ARE POSSIBLE WITH GOD!

It was 1950. We had just finished a week of evangelistic
meetings in the surroundings of Newcastle in the north
of England. The rest of our team had gone home for the
summer holidays; only my friend and I had remained
behind. We had to wait in order to board a cargo ship
which would take us from England to Holland as 'working passengers'. It was not the first time that I had
crossed the North Sea on board a cargo ship: washing

dishes, peeling potatoes, cleaning the vegetables, stoking the ship's furnaces, being a general dog's-body.

I had to ring the head-office of the shipping company in order to find out from which port 'our ship' would sail. I was told the ship would leave from Middlesbrough at noon that same day. It was impossible for us even by a fast train from Newcastle to reach the ship in time. So my friend and I simply knelt down and prayed a simple prayer: 'Lord, if it is Thy will that we should go to Holland, please hold back this ship until we get there'. We hastily completed the packing of our suitcases and sped to the railway station. But before purchasing our tickets for the train journey, seeing that by this time the station clock pointed to 11.30 a.m., I rang the shipping company once more to tell them we were sorry but that we could not possibly manage to get to the ship in time. 'O, Mr. Bruins', said the voice on the phone 'I have got good news for you; the ship has been delayed for 5 hours'. I write this account 30 years later, but I am sure that I must have shouted 'Hallelujah' at this amazing answer to prayer.

We arrived at the quay and found our cargo-boat. Climbing on board, it looked deserted. But then we found that three men were there: the engineer, his sailor-son, and the mate. The latter did not know me and asked what we wanted. So we told him why we were there. 'You know', he said, 'this tub is one of the most immoral I have ever sailed on'. I told him of my experience on other boats of the same company I had sailed on which were just as bad. But then I added that we were Christians, and that we were convinced we had a message for the entire crew, if they would but accept it. He just roared with laughter and left us to settle into our bunks.

At about 5 p.m. the remainder of the 12 man crew were still not there, neither was Captain Smith. We heard them return about 9 p.m., all quite drunk. They could hardly stand upright, and climbing aboard, all went straight to their bunks, except the captain. He told me to follow him down to the galley. We already knew each other from previous voyages. By 10 p.m. we were outside the harbour and by midnight well away on the North Sea. About midnight Captain Smith suddenly said to me: 'Come along with me to the bridge'. We found the sober mate and seaman up there. The seaman was standing behind the great wheel turning it now to the left and then to the right.

'Just show him how to steer the ship' Captain Smith said to the man. And so it happened that on that dark night on the North Sea I had my first lesson in navigation.

After having watched me handle the great helm for ten minutes or so, the two sober men left us for their bunks, and so I remained behind on that bridge with a drunken captain. What an impossible situation I found myself in now! The light shone brightly over the compass in front of me whilst the rest of the bridge was enveloped in darkness, filled with the snoring of the captain. Then suddenly Captain Smith would wake up and tell me that he was not the captain of this ship. 'You have a Captain, you told me, let Him help you now', he said. We had had talks in the past and Captain Smith knew the Gospel; he had two children in the Salvation Army. But he cared for nothing. How helpless I felt that dark night! 'Who am I, Lord? Please help me to steer this ship safely' was my constant prayer. And He who had spoken to Moses, also stood by me, and said: 'Certainly I will be with thee.' (Exd 3:12).

Then came to my mind on that bridge another verse, which the Lord had given me in 1949 when He had called me to follow Him: 'Have not I commanded thee? Be strong and of a good courage; be not afraid, neither be thou dismayed: for the Lord thy God is with thee whithersoever thou goest' (Josh 1:9). At 4 a.m. the mate and the seaman returned to the bridge and how perfectly amazed they were to find that we were still dead on course. A miracle indeed! One of the things that I learned from this experience was: how do we react in a moment of crisis? do we panic, or trust in our own wisdom and self-sufficiency, or do we flee to the Lord? We may find ourselves suddenly placed in an 'impossible situation' – shall we not be able to face it in fellowship with Him?

That reminds me of another experience. The missionary society head-quarters in London had written to ask me to come and start my probationary period with them on Monday, July 6th. I had prayed much about this important matter of going to London, and the Lord had given me peace in my heart. It seemed that guidance through His precious Word, His peace in my heart and circumstances all pointed in one direction – that I had His approval to go to London. But I still needed ten guilders to complete my fare from The Hague via Hook of Holland-Harwich to London. It was Friday evening. My cases were already packed for Monday morning. I kept on saying to the Lord: 'Please, Lord, I still need ten guilders', and the Lord kept on saying to me.' Have not I told you to go?' I had to learn that His Word of promise is as good as a ten guilder banknote. Saturday morning – I still did not have that ten guilders, and so I went and bought a ticket to Ostende in Belgium, changing my route. No doubt somewhere on the way the Lord would provide the means to cross the Channel.

And so on Monday morning I went to the railway station in The Hague with mixed feelings; I still needed those ten guilders. Some of my friends were there waiting on the platform to see me off. Standing there waiting for the train I prayed in desperation: 'Dear Lord, I still do not have the money'. In the distance the train was now approaching the station. Suddenly one of my friends came up to me and said: 'I could not sleep all night. It seemed the Lord was saying to me, "Give Cor Bruins five guilders." Here they are'. How I praised the Lord for those five guilders. I thanked my friend for this wonderful gift. But it still was not enough and I cried to the Lord: 'Lord, I still need five guilders more.' The train now came to a halt and I had to get in. As I put my right foot inside the train, suddenly another friend came up to me and said, 'Cor, the Lord seems to say to me that I must give you five guilders. Here they are'. Unforgettable moments! Not only did the Lord know my needs, but the added miracle was that there were two of His children, independently of each other, ready to obey His gentle leading. Indeed, all things are possible with God!

Moses certainly had to be convinced of this. Just think of the immense task of leading a mass of people, some think probably about 2 million, with cattle, through an empty and barren desert. Unbelievers asked the question: 'Can God furnish a table in the wilderness?' (Ps 78:19). Do we believe that God can still do that today? We have become so used to a welfare state with social security, that this kind of life of faith seems very remote to most of us. But God has not changed. If we truly desire to do His will, we need never be afraid that He will not take care of everything in our lives.

One summer I worked as gardener at the missionary college where I was a student. All my money had finished; I literally did not have a single 'penny' to buy a stamp to send a letter to my parents in Holland. There were several things I desperately needed. I fell on my knees by the side of my bed and poured out my heart before the Lord. I pleaded the precious promise of His Word: Matthew 6:33 and Philippians 4:19 in the wonderful Name of the Lord Jesus.

Having thanked Him that He had heard me, I got up from my knees. Five minutes later I stood by the door of the principal and saw on a little table a letter addressed to me. It had an English postage stamp on it. Whoever knew me here in England? I tore open the envelope and took out the letter which read as follows:

Dear brother,

You probably do not know who we are, but when we visited your College recently the principal mentioned your name to us. From that moment we have prayed for you every day. This morning the Lord seemed to say to my wife and me: 'Send one pound sterling to Bruins'. We herewith enclose this little gift from the Lord to you with our best wishes in the Lord.

It is in moments like these that you begin to experience the truth of the Bible which says: 'And it shall come to pass, that before they call, I will answer; and while they are yet speaking, I will hear' (Is 65:24). This is true with regard to our material needs as well as with our spiritual and physical needs. The whole history of the life of Moses shows us his unshakeable confidence in God, never wavering in spite of the most impossible situations. No wonder that God spoke with Moses 'mouth to mouth (face to face)'. (Num 12:8).

6

PAUL – THE GREATEST MISSIONARY OF ALL TIMES

No doubt the apostle Paul is quite unique both in his person and in his service for the Lord. He had so many qualities which made him a great man of God, spiritual as well as natural qualities. We can all learn a tremendous amount from the apostle Paul. He himself says to us: 'Be ye followers of me, even as I also am of Christ' (1 Cor 11:1).

In the chapters which follow we propose to consider some of the qualities of the great apostle, and thereby seek to learn from him. Because there is such a mass of material we propose to deal with it by dividing our subject matter into three main sections; Spiritual qualities, Moral qualities and Practical qualities.

Let us not become discouraged with the thought of what Paul was and what poor creatures we are. The same Holy Spirit who indwelt and worked through the apostle, also indwells and seeks to work through us. We all have the responsibility, in dependence upon the Lord, to develop qualities which the Holy Spirit can use to the glory of our Lord Jesus Christ. This is exactly what the apostle Peter writes about: 'giving all diligence, add to your faith virtue; and to virtue knowledge; and to knowledge temperance; and to temperance patience; and to patience godliness; and to godliness brotherly kindness;

and to brotherly kindness love.' (2 Pet 1:5–7).

Spiritual gifts can only come from God, but the development of spiritual and moral characteristics is the result of an ever deepening devotion, surrender and whole hearted obedience to the Lord Jesus. That is *our* responsibility! Christ-likeness does not take place in us *haphazardly,* against our will. It must be our passionate longing to be utterly for Him, or as someone expressed it: 'my utmost for His highest'. But how shall we be able to realise this?

Spiritual qualities

Knowledge of the scriptures

Saul of Tarsus was the son of orthodox parents who undoubtedly brought him up in the nurture and admonition of the God of Israel. In accordance with Jewish tradition baby Saul was circumcised on the eighth day (Phil 3:5). At the age of three he would be given a tasseled garment, probably worn at religious festive occasions, which would teach him to love the things of the Lord. At the age of five he would begin memorising all the five books of Moses, and of course from these learn to read and write. At the age of twelve boys were taken to Jerusalem to attend the Passover feast and visit the Temple. At the age of fifteen Saul most probably left for Jerusalem to continue his education. As we know from himself, he became a student of the great teacher Gamaliel (Acts 22:3).

From the above we may quite safely conclude that before his conversion to Christ Paul had a considerable knowledge of Old Testament writings. It must also be quite clear to us all that Paul did not obtain this vast knowledge 'automatically'! No doubt he must have put a great amount of concentrated effort into his 'Bible-study' to gather this knowledge. Later he encouraged another young Bible student with these words: 'Study to shew thyself approved unto God, a workman that needeth not to be ashamed, rightly dividing the word of truth' (2 Tim 2:15).

We can trace his vast knowledge of the Old Testament writings in his own writings in the New Testament. It was the indispensable foundation upon which by the Holy Spirit his inspired epistles were written. How indispensable it is also for us to know the Bible, to be able to express ourselves 'biblically'. We need to know God's Word in order to be able to withstand the onslaughts of the enemy. Our blessed Lord Jesus said three times to Satan: 'It is written', and the enemy had to give ground and yield to the power of the precious Word of God (see Matt 4:1–10).

As true believers we must be able to use 'the sword of the Spirit, which is the Word of God' (Eph 6:17). How much more is a thorough knowledge of the Bible required of those who aspire to serve the Lord! Do we really know the Word of God? Although much helpful material has already been published on the subject, it is perhaps useful to give here some guide-lines as to how to study the Bible with the most profit. We distinguish:

1. Personal Bible-study.
2. Communal Bible-study in fellowship with others, and this can be done within the frame-work of our local assembly:
   a. in the weekly Bible-studies, or
   b. through the ministry of a Bible teacher, or
   c. conferences for the building up of spiritual life
   d. other opportunities which present themselves
   e. through reading commentaries, books, expositions, writing etc.

Now some hints to methods of Bible-study. There is first of all the so-called *synthetical* method of Bible-study; by this is meant that method whereby the various parts are viewed together, are seen in their relation to one another, and are regarded as constituting a whole.

1. The obvious variety in the contents of the Bible is noted:
   a. Legislative: the five books of Moses, also called the Pentateuch, (these are partly Historical books).
   b. Executive: twelve books from Joshua to Esther (these are also Historical books).
   c. Poetry: Psalms and Song of Solomon (these books are called Didactical, meaning teaching, educative).
   d. Wisdom: Job, Proverbs and Ecclesiastes (also called Didactical).
   e. Prophetical: 5 'Major', and 12 'Minor' prophets.

In the New Testament we have:
   a. Christ: the 4 Gospels (Historical).
   b. The Church: The Acts (Historical).
   c. Paulinic writings: 14 epistles (Didactical).
   d. General writings: 7 epistles (Didactical).
   e. Prophetical writings: The Revelation.

2. Next we see the obvious unity of the 66 books of the Bible which is due to the fact that Christ is its sole object and subject.

3. The obvious agreement between the Old Testament and the New Testament writings is seen when we place the above five sub-divisions parallel to each other and so compare them.

Secondly there is the so-called *analytical* method of Bible study whereby books and details are separately regarded. We move here from the specific to the general; it is the 'microscopic method'.

If we study the books of the Bible separately, we must repeatedly ask ourselves the following questions: What is the background: place, time, goal, circumstance? What is the character of the book? How can the book be sub-divided?

If we study and try to explain separate texts, we ought

to ask ourselves the following questions.

1. In which way must this text be explained? Is the character of this text typical, allegorical, figurative, spiritual, metaphorical, symbolical or literal, or prophetical, etc. etc.?

2. Can the text be placed in any of the time-periods of the history of redemption? For example: the period from Adam to the Fall; from Adam to the Flood; from Noah to Abraham; from Moses to the Cross of Christ; during the period of the presence of the Church on earth, or after the Rapture of the Church?

3. Has the text any connection with a covenant? Which covenant? The promise to Adam? the covenant with Noah? with Abraham? with the nation of Israel in the promised land? with David? with the New Covenant?

4. Is there a setting aside of the old order, and the introduction of a new order and new principles? Is it dated before Christ's birth, death and resurrection, or after it? Is it dated at the inauguration of the Church period or at the end of its presence on earth?

Then there is also the study of: subjects, persons, doctrines, miracles, parables, types etc. etc.

We have therefore the duty to 'search the scriptures' (Jn 5:39), to 'meditate' (Josh 1:8), to 'compare' (1 Cor 2:13), and prayerfully to try to put into practice in our daily lives what we have learned. It is a very good habit always to carry about a small note-book. Make notes of everything you hear in meetings, and of your own personal Bible-study and reading of literature that will help you to better understand the Word of God. Remember this fundamental rule: never judge the Bible, but allow the Bible to examine and judge you. And do not forget: before you open that precious book PRAY. Ask for divine illumination, guidance and help. Believe in the absolute authority and truth of the Bible.

At this point some of my readers may ask whether

Bible study would be helped by formal theological or missionary training at a college or Bible-school. Let me try to answer this question with another question. What do you think you can learn at a Bible- or missionary school or college that you cannot also learn by self-study, outside the walls of such an institute? My personal and humble opinion is (having myself in fact followed such a course) that it is not necessary and in some cases even dangerous to enroll as a student in some such institute. In ordinary life there are many who, besides their daily work, follow special courses by correspondence, or self-study or through the 'open university' at home, and obtain the required knowledge and qualifications. Of course, it will probably take more time. A 2 or 3 year study at an institute full time naturally becomes more drawn out when it is followed along side one's daily occupation.

The subjects which are generally taught at a Bible- or missionary college are:

1. Disciplined Bible-study: research (the who and what of hermeneutics, which is defined as the scholarly attempt to clarify principles pertinent to an adequate understanding and interpretation of texts as well as monuments), exegesis: exposition of scripture etc.

2. Homiletics: the art of preaching.

3. Languages: mostly Hebrew and Greek.

4. World-religions: also sects, philosophy and biblical psychology.

5. Missionary strategy.

6. Study of cultures and customs.

7. Practical evangelism, such as open-air preaching, literature evangelism, home and hospital visitation, child-evangelism, youthwork etc.

The real qualifications are spiritual, not academic. There are numerous examples of true and famous men and women who have served Christ both at home and abroad without having had any formal theological or missionary training. Our advice is, if you have never been to a theological or missionary training institute, do not seek it, or think that without such training you cannot serve the Lord. You are in the school of God where the Holy Spirit is your teacher. He knows what equipment you will need for any future service you may be called upon to do for your Mater, and He will give you His enabling. Seek only to be in the centre of His will and be teachable.

James Hudson Taylor, pioneer missionary to China, whom God greatly used for His glory, and who founded the China Inland Mission, said that to be a missionary one would need the following equipment:

1. A life yielded to God, controlled by the Holy Spirit (Rom 6:13, 16, 19).

2. A restful trust in God for the supply of all needs (Phil 4:11, 19).

3. A sympathetic spirit and willingness to take a lowly place (Phil 2:7; Mk 10:45).

4. Tact in dealing with people and adaptation to circumstances (Matt 10:16).

5. Zeal in service and steadfastness in discouragements (Acts 27:21–25).

6. Love for communion with God and for the study of His Word (Ps 119:15, 16, 97, 129).

7. Some experience and blessing in the Lord's work at home.

8. A healthy body and a vigorous mind (2 Cor 11:24–28; 2 Tim 2:15; 4:13.)

Spiritual power

Only when we are willing to bow to God's word in all humility, and accept its absolute authority over our lives, shall we experience its power. To obey that word of God and allow it to guide us in the smallest details and daily circumstances of our lives is conditional to proving its power. 'Finally, my brethren, be strong in the Lord, and in the power of his might' (Eph 6:10).

If we read the Bible and study it merely in order to increase our knowledge, perhaps with the secret ambition of appearing more learned and knowledgeable than others, we will not experience the spiritual power of the Word. There is nothing more spiritually sterile than an intellectual grasp of the Word. Someone has well defined what I am trying to say: Scholarship baffles, learning bewilders, efficiency chills, aggressiveness antagonizes, but a winsome spirituality draws men to Christ. This is only possible when the word of Christ dwells in us richly (Col 3:16).

Spirituality and godliness are the results of deep meditation upon God's word and thoughts and the consequent putting into practice of what one has understood. The power to put that knowledge into practice is given through prayer. Prayer before reading and studying, seeking to understand what we read, asking the Lord to help us put it into practice: that gives spiritual power. The energy of the spiritual life therefore is prayer. We see this energy and the power of prayer in the life of the apostle Paul. Read through his epistles and letters, study the book of the Acts, and you will see that Paul did not consider prayer as something optional, but as utterly essential and vital.

His prayers were not formalised, yet they were not incoherent or aimless. Sometimes it was a quiet prayer, at other times full of fervour and with deep sentiments. He never seemed to stop praying (see 2 Tim 1;3). Prayer was his way of what we might call 'the practice of the presence of the Lord'. This does not mean that we need to be on our knees all day long! The fact that Paul maintained this constant attitude of prayerful dependence shows how conscious he was of the necessity to pray for everyone and everything. It was his continual habit, and so it became a way of life to him. He did not only pray, but also always added thanksgiving.

Most of his recorded prayers in scripture are concerning persons and their various needs and necessities. We can safely say therefore that the secret of Paul's dynamic spiritual life was prayer. And the effectiveness of his prayers was his complete confidence in the Lord and His love, wisdom and power. Through prayer the most impossible becomes possible.

This man of God, this man of prayer, did realise nevertheless that he needed the prayers of others: 'Brethren, pray for us' he says in 1 Thess 5.25, and 'Now I beseech you, brethren, for the Lord Jesus Christ's sake, and for the love of the Spirit, that ye strive together with me in your prayers to God for me' (Rom 15:30). He was utterly convinced of the power and efficacy of prayer, and he felt that the prayers of his fellow-believers were for him an essential and decisive element in his service for Christ (see Phil 1:19).

This 'quiet time' of meditating upon the Bible, and prayer, is essential for all Christians who today desire to stand against the current of this world's systems and all satanic powers. David found that the early hours of the morning were the most suitable for his 'quiet time' (Ps 5:3, 4): 'My voice shalt thou hear in the morning, O Lord; in the morning will I direct my prayer unto thee, and will look up'. Perhaps for some of us it is not possible to arrange a period of quiet time in the morning; we do not have to be legalistic on this point, as long as we try to arrange some definite time during the day to be quiet with Him. That is the most important thing. It may be some of us are a little disorganised, but most of us can always find time for something we really desperately want to do. It is through prayer and the reading of God's word that we receive our daily 'guidance' and direction from God, even if it is only a deep sense of His presence and peace.

Having mentioned guidance.... This is a very important matter about which so many of God's children are very confused. Without clear guidance from the Lord there cannot be any spiritual power either, because we are not sure that what we are doing is His will.

The way in which the apostle Paul received his guidance may serve as an illustration and encouragement for us all. Please turn to Acts 16:6–11. Here we read that Paul and his companions on their second missionary journey were forbidden of the Holy Spirit to preach the word in Asia. Did Paul say: 'If I cannot go there, what else shall I do?' Definitely not. We read: 'After they were come to Mysia, they assayed to go into Bithynia: but the Spirit suffered them not' (v.7). That was the second time the door was slammed shut in their faces. No doubt Paul must have prayed much that night! And then the answer came. At last clear guidance was given. Paul was completely convinced, and therefore we read: 'And after he had seen the vision, immediately we endeavoured to go into Macedonia, assuredly gathering that the Lord had called us for to preach the gospel unto them' (v.10).

My friend and I had received an invitation to preach the Word in Antwerp (Belgium). We had spread the invitation before the Lord in prayer and asked Him for His guidance. He gave us deep peace, and we knew that it was His will for us to accept the invitation. But I had no money for the train-fare from The Hague to Antwerp (which is about 80 miles to the south). We would leave on Saturday morning from the main railway station in The Hague. It was the night before (Friday) that my friend asked me: 'Well, Cor, do you have the money for the train-fare?' 'No', I said, 'but I am sure the Lord will provide. Let us meet at the entrance to the station tomorrow'.

On Saturday morning I awoke and started to think at once of that journey to Belgium. I got out of bed and prayed to the Lord. Then it seemed as if a voice said to me: 'A single journey by tramway to the railway station costs 12 cents, and a return 15 cents; you ought to buy a return and save yourself money because you are not going to have enough money to get back home from the station. You do not have your train-fare to Belgium, and so you will be coming back home again from the station'. 'No', I said: 'I believe that the Lord has called me to go to Antwerp, and that I must get there tonight, how I do not know, but I will not doubt. I shall buy a single journey on the tramway to the railway station'.

Having made this decision and having thanked the Lord for His provision, I hastily finished my breakfast. My friend was waiting for me in the entrance hall of the station.

'Have you got the money now for your fare?' he asked. 'No', I said, 'but I want you to go on ahead; I shall follow a bit later'. So my friend left with the train. There I stood alone in the hall. 'What must I do now, Lord?' The Lord said: 'With that money your mother gave you for a cup of coffee, take another tram and go to the outskirts of the town and stand by the motorway to Rotterdam and wait'.

I had only waited a short while when a car drew up and the driver, opening the window, called out: 'Where do you want to go?' 'To Rotterdam', I said. 'All right, get in'. On arrival in Rotterdam the driver let me out in the centre of the town, right beside the international motorway to the south. I prayed: 'Lord, what am I to do now?' Then I noticed a Jaguar car with a GB registration which had stopped in a lay-by. 'That Englishman has lost his way' I said to myself. 'Can I perhaps be of any assistance to you, sir?' I said in English. 'Yes, please, come sit beside me; look at this map. But where are you going?' 'O, me, I have to go to Antwerp'. 'Splendid! I am just ending my holiday on the Continent. I have been all over the place, and am heading for home now. I'll come with you to Antwerp'.

The next couple of hours were spent in a serious conversation with the Englishman on how one can be saved for eternity. He became deeply impressed and under conviction of the Holy Spirit. Then, before we realised it, we had actually arrived in Antwerp, right in front of the main railway station. I was getting out of the car, when my host bashfully said: 'I say, as I am leaving for England tomorrow, I do not know what to do with all these loose foreign coins I have collected. Do you think you could perhaps do something with them?' And so he emptied his pocketsful of money into my empty hands!

Very soon after, I stood in front of the door of my lodgings for that night, and rang the bell. The door opened and there stood my friend from The Hague who had only just arrived by train himself. He looked at me with unbelieving eyes thinking I was a ghost. Then I told him my amazing story. God had seen this lonely man in his car on holiday and wanted him to hear the message of salvation by faith in the Lord Jesus Christ. 'How then shall they call on him in whom they have not believed? and how shall they believe in him of whom they have not heard? and how shall they hear without a preacher? and how shall they preach, except they be sent?' (Rom 10:14, 15).

Back in The Hague the Lord did not give me my train-fare because He wanted me to meet this Englishman. God had other plans: not by train but in a lovely fast Jaguar I was to travel, and so have opportunity to tell a thirsty soul the message of salvation.

The question naturally arises as to how one can be sure that one is taking the right decision? How can one be sure of being in God's will? First of all: God expects from us that we shall desire to know His will and do it: 'Wherefore be ye not unwise, but understanding what the will of the Lord is' (Eph 5:17). The Bible tells us that God's will can be known: 'The meek shall he guide in judgment: and the meek will he teach his way' (Ps 25:9).

But we must realise that God will only reveal His will to those who are prepared to obey Him, who really long to know Him. The apostle Paul shows us very clearly the conditions for knowing God's will, in Romans 12:1, 2: 'I beseech you therefore, brethren, by the mercies of God, that ye present your bodies a living sacrifice, holy, acceptable unto God, which is your intelligent service. And be not conformed to this world: but be ye transformed by the renewing of your mind, that ye may prove what is that good, and acceptable, and perfect, will of God'. Notice the conditions: complete surrender of Him of our bodies, our minds and our wills!

God's will is always the best for us. The realisation of that will of God is a very personal and individual matter. His will is related to such mundane things as our holidays, business travels, marriage, or whether we shall remain single, our health, our past, present and future.

If we have to take a decision, it is good to ask ourselves the following questions.

1. Am I willing to do God's will? 'If any man will *do* his will, he shall *know* of the doctrine whether it be of God' (Jn 7:17).

2. Have I paid attention to what God's word tells me with regard to my particular problem? God does show us His will sometimes through the reading of His word. We ought to read it therefore faithfully and attentively. God's Spirit will never lead us into anything that is contrary to the teaching of His own word.

3. Have I made it a matter of earnest prayer? Indeed, can I pray about it? Have I asked the Lord to reveal to me His will clearly so that I may discern it?

4. Have I examined my motives with regard to this matter of guidance in this particular problem? In other words, am I sure that what I want Him to do for me is for His glory?

5. Am I prepared to use my God-given common sense? Remember what we read earlier in Romans 12,

that the Holy Spirit daily renews our minds (i.e. under-standing).

6. Do I have real deep peace with the decision I have taken? 'And let the peace of Christ rule in your hearts, to the which also ye are called' (Col 3:15). To maintain that you know God's will in a particular matter and meanwhile you are terribly restless and fretful concerning the deci-sion you have taken, is of course nonsense. We are only deceiving ourselves. When God has clearly shown His will, one of the signs is that we have the peace that passeth all understanding in our hearts. (Phil 4:7).

7. Have you talked things over with another spiritual believer, and asked his or her advice? Remember: 'in the multitude of counsellors there is safety' (Prov 11:14).

8. Have you considered your present circumstances? What do they tell you? Is there an open door or a closed door? It may be that you are knocking on the wrong door. Sometimes God closes one door in order to open another. At other times a door may open which never-theless presents many problems and difficulties, but this does not necessarily mean that this is not of God:' For a great door and effectual is opened unto me, and there are many adversaries' (1 Cor 16:9).

9. Am I flexible and pliable? It may be that in the past you have taken a certain decision which you were sure was God's will. Quite possibly it was God's will for you then! But we must remember that there is what we might call: a. God's relative or permissive will, and: b. His absolute and ultimate purpose. Remain open therefore for re-direction if necessary. Do not become fixed and rigid and unpliable. Do not forget that 'we know in part', imperfectly (1 Cor 13:9), and that God may sometimes reveal His will progressively and at different stages.

Moral qualities

A disciplined lifestyle

'I therefore so run, not as uncertainly; so fight I, not as one that beateth the air: But I keep under my body, and bring it into subjection' (1 Cor 9:26, 27).

'All things are lawful unto me, but all things are not expedient: all things are lawful for me, but I will not be brought under the power of any' (1 Cor 6:12).

'But the fruit of the Spirit is...self-control' (Gal 5:22, 23).

We all know that we live in a permissive society. 'God is dead', they say. There is no God! Therefore nobody is obliged to give an account of what he does, or has done in the past. There is no absolute moral standard for behaviour, so we are told. Everybody does his own thing as he thinks best in the circumstances!

'Liberty', is the motto of today. Nobody tells *me* what to do, and what not to do, is what men say. Or in the words of Psalm 2:3: 'Let us break their bands asunder, and cast away their cords from us'. We do not want to be restrained! This philosophy is widespread and openly taught and accepted by the majority. No doubt this is the reason for the chaos, which borders on anarchy, in which we live. We see it in the marriage relationship between husband and wife, between parents and children, at school and in society.

How does the believer determine his or her attitude in the midst of this desperate and chaotic society? It is very sad to have to say that many Christians have also been contaminated by this social plague. But for all those who want to please God, who want to follow the Lord Jesus, and who desire the Holy Spirit to lead them, for all those who accept the Bible as the absolute and God-given standard by which to regulate conduct, and who are willing to submit to that Word, it is gloriously possible to resist and remain immovable in this chaos.

Undoubtedly, those who are thus determined will not find it easy going. But remember, a dead fish does not find it difficult to float with the stream and current; it is the energetic and vivacious salmon who can swim against the strong currents and even jump the rapids higher and higher to get to its goal. A nominal Christian has no life, and of course will join the crowd and is influenced by the movements and philosophies of today. But what about a real Christian? Many believers alas, who have been born again, do not know in experience the power of the Holy Spirit in their daily lives. Unfortunately they are therefore also easily influenced by the present day philosophy and outlook on life. They are what we might call 'worldly', that is they are acting exactly like people who live only for *this* world.

Now of course discipleship has to do with discipline. Without discipline we cannot be good disciples. Today more than ever the true believer ought to realise the necessity for discipline, order and self-control.

Self-control: For most of us this is a strange and old fashioned word. It sounds really prim. Yet the bible tells us that self-control is one of the watermarks of the genuineness of a child of God, and a positive sign of the fact that the Holy Spirit is in control of his life (Gal 5:22, 23).

We must however carefully distinguish between, on the one hand, fanaticism (which is manifested by excesses, by a slavish submission to rules and laws, and is commonly called legalism), and on the other hand the obvious fruit of the indwelling of God's Spirit in the believer which manifests itself in self-control.

The self-control in the life of the child of God becomes apparent the moment he wakes up in the morning. That dreadful alarm-clock which does not cease to ring and irritate me whilst it shouts at me that it is high time to get up! Warning me that if I linger there will be no time left for reading my Bible and prayer. Yes, but I am still so tired and sleepy. 'Yet a little sleep, a little slumber, a little folding of the hands to sleep...' (Prov 6:10; 24:33). And then we wake up suddenly with a shock, heart thumping away. Now we have overslept. No more time unfortunately for reading or praying. We decide to take a little time for that later at work during the midday interval. But the devil will see to it that we never do get time. And, would you believe it, that day we have to stay late at work. So we get back home late, and of course we are tired out. No more energy left to devote time and to concentrate on a little Bible study. We determine not to let this happen again. But tomorrow comes and we fail again. And so we just struggle and fail miserably. We always excuse ourselves. That is the reason why there will never be a change. As a matter of fact, if we are really honest with ourselves, we do not like this self-discipline, we do not want self-control. It is far too difficult and costly, and we would rather be self-indulgent.

It is indeed remarkable that those men whom God could use were all people who seemed habitually to be early risers. Look at Abraham for instance (in Gen 22:3), and Jacob (in Gen 28:18); and Moses (in Ex 24:4); and Joshua (in Josh 3:1); and Gideon (in Judg 6:38); and Samuel (in 1 Sam 15:12); and David (in 1 Sam 17:20); and Job (in Job 1:5); and very especially look at the Lord Jesus Christ (Mk 1:35).

Now that we have mentioned sleeping and waking up, what shall we say about eating and drinking, and having a healthy appetite? Is it good or bad to indulge in these? It is of course quite normal for our bodies to have appetites. It is normal to feel hungry. It is normal also to have sexual desires, although there are believers who are almost obsessed with these desires, and when these are not controlled, it becomes lust! Others are not much bothered about it, by the grace of God.

There are some who are slaves to smoking, drinking

alcoholic drinks and other beverages, eating sweets, and
we could give a long list of things to which we can all
become enslaved. These things in themselves are not
necessarily sinful. With proper use and with self-control
they may be quite legitimate and neutral. The apostle
Paul says: 'I know, and am persuaded by the Lord Jesus,
that there is nothing unclean of itself: but to him that
esteemeth anything to be unclean, to him it is unclean'
(see Rom 14:14).

This does not mean however that as long as I do not
think that a thing is unclean, it is therefore not sinful to
indulge in it. Whatever the Bible forbids and condemns,
should be taboo for the believer. But if we have no
chapter or verse that would be decisive for determining a
certain line of conduct, then we ought to submit ourselves to the discipline and guidance of the Holy Spirit
and apply the law of brotherly love. Would we be prepared to give up some cherished habits or things, should
the circumstances require it of us, or when it becomes a
matter of being able to render a positive witness, rather
than giving offence?

All countries have their traditions and customs, and
those who serve the Lord in foreign lands do well to
remember this. They should always be ready to adapt
themselves to the circumstances of the environment in
which they find themselves.

There exists for instance quite a difference of opinion
amongst believers about smoking and drinking alcoholic
beverages. A brother from the Middle East attended a
conference once in Europe. He shared his lodgings with
a European brother. Without so much as giving it a
moment's consideration whether he would give offence
to our brother from the Middle East, our European
brother enveloped his fellow believer in a thick cloud of
cigar smoke and at the same time quenched his thirst
with a large glass of beer! Do you not think that it is high
time we all started reading and studying the contents of

Romans 14 again?

If you, in the Middle East (I just fix on that part of the world with which I am personally better acquainted) invite a Muslim to a meal, you would not be so tactless as to serve him pork! For you and me it may be perfectly normal to eat pork, but for another it would be sinful to eat it.

A brother in Europe once said aloud: 'I can thank God for a fine cigar'. I am willing to accept the sincerity of this brother, but I would like to say to him: 'It is good neither to eat flesh, nor to drink wine, nor any thing whereby thy brother stumbleth, or is offended, or is made weak. Hast thou faith? have it to thyself before God' (Rom 14:21, 22).

Are you thinking of serving the Lord at home or abroad? Please remember that men will watch and observe you, and be careful with the sometimes over-sensitive consciences of others. Ask the Lord to give you self-control, and power through the Holy Spirit to be willing to sacrifice and accept self-denial.

Sexual appetite is a normal constituent of our human bodies as God Himself has created them. The appetite is not sinful, but may become an instrument influenced by the 'sin that dwells in us' (see Rom 7:17), and so its power and potential are abused. Our bodies are not sinful either, but indwelling sin can use our bodies and our members to perform sinful acts. Paul says some very important things about our bodies in 1 Corinthians 6:13–20.

1. He says that the body is for the Lord, and the Lord is for the body (v.13), and that our bodies are the members of Christ (v.15). We ought therefore not to degrade our bodies or abuse them in an unworthy manner.

2. God attaches great value to our bodies and will therefore raise them by His own power. Our present physical bodies are as it were the seedlings for our future glorified bodies, which will be like unto our Lord Jesus' glorified body (v.14).

3. The Holy Spirit honours the body by making it His residence and temple (v.19).

4. We ought therefore to glorify God with and in our physical bodies with all their potential, and this we are only able to do when we offer up these bodies as a living sacrifice, holy, acceptable unto God.

When we are willing to surrender our bodies into the hands of the Lord, we will then receive a correct insight as to how to use, or it may be sublimate, our sexual appetite.

We will then also hand over this legitimate urge to the discipline and control of the Holy Spirit. We will be given discernment and begin to see things in their true context, as through the eyes of the Lord, whether it is in the matter of falling in love, getting engaged, getting married, or remaining unmarried, having children or remaining childless, when to use or to refuse the gift of our sexuality. Everything will then be considered as a gift from God which we may either yield back to Him, or thankfully accept from Him and enjoy. 'Marriage is honourable in all, and the bed undefiled' (Heb 13:4).

We all realise how much we need self-control in this area: 'every one of you should know how to possess his vessel in sanctification and honour; not in lustful passion as the heathen do...' (1 Thess 4:4, 5).

In other words: if marriage is the normal thing for most of us, and sexual urges and desires within the marriage bond a gift from God, this does not give us the licence to abuse it or abandon ourselves wholly to it.

Does anyone ask how we can control this urge? The answer to this question is found in v.8 of 1 Thessalonians 4: 'If anyone refuses to live by these rules he is not disobeying the rules of men but of God who gives his Holy Spirit to you' (paraphrased). It is the Holy Spirit who gives us the power to exercise self-control.

There are believers who are much distressed by unclean thoughts. How can they find deliverance from these? I believe the answer is found in Philippians 4:8: 'And now, brothers,...fix your thoughts on what is true and good and right. Think about things that are pure and lovely, and dwell on the fine, good things in others. Think about all you can praise God for and be glad about' (paraphrased). To be occupied with the Lord Jesus and his interest, and to memorize scriptures day by day, that is the remedy for unclean thoughts. It is so easy for any one to let things slip and go, to relax vigilance and self-discipline, especially when tired physically or mentally. Those who have lived, or still live in countries with a hot or tropical climate know from experience how a hot and moist temperature has an exceedingly debilitating effect. It is very easy in such circumstances to give up fighting and rather let things take their course. You just do not have the energy, or the will-power left to resist.

We have to know how to *flee* sinful lusts (2 Tim 2:22); we must not act as if these lusts do not exist, but we must yield ourselves continually into the hands of the Lord. He gives us power to exercise self-control. But we must determine to: '....so fight I, not as one that beateth the air: but I keep under my body, and bring it into subjection...', as Paul says in 1 Corinthians 9:26, 27.

Clothing: True Christianity is very practical and touches every aspect of our internal and external lives. What we believe definitely determines our conduct. If we believe that our bodies are temples of the Holy Spirit, it will make us reflect as to how we adorn that temple. If a man believes that he evolved from an animal and that he is an animal, he will also behave like one – a fact which we witness all around us. It should therefore not be thought inappropriate by my reader if we spend a little time discussing self-control and self-discipline in the realm of clothing. Surely we would all agree that self-control ought also to be manifested in the way in which we dress, or 'undress' our bodies. Yes, even in such mundane matters as what to wear we need the help and guidance of the Holy Spirit.

As believers, (both male and female), we ought indeed to ask ourselves whether by this or that way of dressing ourselves we do not give offence to others.

On the so-called missionfield it is also very important to remember that we do not give offence to the nationals by the way we might, perhaps unconsciusly, go too far in dressing ourselves 'lightly' because of the heat.

We should never dress ourselves in such a way as to become conspicuous. We become conspicuous when we overdress ourselves, but also on the other hand when we dress really slovenly and look unkempt. Neither is good. If by outward apparel we start drawing attention to ourselves, then Jesus Christ will not be manifested in and through us. We are then achieving the exact opposite of what may perhaps be our sincere desire: that Jesus Christ be glorified in us. It is a fact that brothers as well as sisters in Christ can sin in this respect. Certainly, a brother who teaches or exhorts others and is therefore often in the public eye, ought to be well aware of the above mentioned dangers and seek to avoid them like the plague.

Giving: Next we want to say something about disciplined and responsible stewardship in giving to the Lord. This is not something optional, for in Hebrews 13:16 we read: 'But to do good and to communicate forget not: for with such sacrifices God is well pleased'. It is not so much a question as to how much we give, but rather of how much we keep for ourselves. How much do we give in reality to the Lord or His work, and to all the many needs that surround us?

As a young believer I thought I should give a tithe, the tenth part of everything. Did it not clearly say so in Malachi 3:10: 'Bring ye all the tithes into the storehouse, that there may be meat in mine house, and prove me now herewith, saith the Lord of hosts, if I will not open you the windows of heaven, and pour you out a blessing, that there shall not be room enough to receive it'? Now I can hear somebody say: 'But dear brother, we are no longer under the law; to give tithes or the tenth part was for those under the law'. You are absolutely right my friend, and I entirely agree with you. But before we proceed, may I ask you a question? Seeing that we are now happily no longer hindered or regulated by the law, we are therefore gloriously free to give as much as we like. But does this work out practically in your and my life? Do we in fact give more, or less, than a tenth of our income? Is the fact that we are no longer under the law for us a convenient excuse to give less, rather than a fantastic opportunity to give unstintingly and generously?

The wonderful thing in Christian giving is that it is not a MUST, but a MAY! We may give as much as our hearts allow us, and then we always think of what Paul says in 2 Corinthians 9:6–8: 'He which soweth sparingly shall reap also sparingly; and he which soweth bountifully shall reap also bountifully. Every man according as he purposeth in his heart, so let him give; not grudgingly, or of necessity: for God loveth a cheerful giver. And God is able to make all grace abound toward you; that ye, always having all sufficiency in all things, may abound to every good work'.

Let us imagine for a moment that a believer earns a net monthly salary of £600. Does he in fact immediately set apart at least £60 for the Lord? And if we are not able to affirm with a positive 'Yes', are we convinced that this should change in the near future?

In a certain respect it would perhaps be good with regard to ourselves that we set aside a tenth of our income to the Lord, individually, as a habit, and then, as occasion serves, so as not to let our left hand know what our right hand does, to give over and above in doing good around us. Certainly God's work and His workers would then have all the support they need financially, and two good things would result from our giving – those in need would be helped, and they would overflow with thanks to God.

About thirty years ago I was doing some door to door visiting in a very poor neighbourhood somewhere in the north of the U.K. I had been invited in by a lady living in rather a hovel of a house, and had talked to her about the love of the Saviour. As I was ready to leave, it seemed as if a voice in my heart said to me: 'Give her all you have in your pocket'. That was exactly half-a-crown: all my earthly wealth! The conviction was so overwhelming that I must give her all. The Lord gave me grace to obey. Later that week the Lord gave me back more than I had given away. But I had to learn the lesson that ALL that I am and possess is HIS, not just a tenth!

In 1952 I lived as a student in a London guesthouse. In those days my lodging cost me £2.10 – a week. It happened one week that I did not have enough money to pay my bill, but there was enough in my little box entitled: TENTHS FOR THE LORD. The Lord had to teach me through those circumstances once again that EVERYTHING was His: my shortage was His shortage, and my sufficiency was His sufficiency in that little box. Not only the tenths in that box belonged to Him, but absolutely everything I was and possessed, or lacked. He gave me peace that time and liberty to pay my bill with His tenths, and then I understood the lesson.

But there was yet another lesson I had to learn at this time. I just could not understand that although I was sure I was in the will of the Lord, I nevertheless could not pay my bill. How was this possible: to walk in His will and yet to lack the necessities of life? I had read it very clearly in Philippians 4:19: 'But my God shall supply all your need according to his riches in glory by Christ Jesus'.

I took this wonderful promise to the Lord in prayer, and also that other promise in Matthew 6:33 'But seek ye first the kingdom of God and his righteousness; and all these things shall be added unto you'. But then the Lord pointed out to me vv. 11 and 12 in Philippians 4: '...for I have learned, in whatsoever state I am, therewith to be content. I know both how to be abased, and I know how to abound: every where and in all things I am instructed both to be full and to be hungry, both to abound and to suffer need'. I had never 'seen' these verses before, as I 'saw' them now. Paul, that great servant of God, called by the Lord to do His service, and yet he knew how 'to be hungry' and to 'suffer need'. But why? Now I saw the reason: I also had to learn in whatsoever state I am to be happy and content. It did not mean then, that because I had sufficient and perhaps abundance, therefore my affluence was necessarily a sign that I was in the will of God. And vice versa, if I had need and lacked necessities, that was not necessarily a sign that I was not in the will of God. The most important thing is to be sure that He is with us in all circumstances. Then I can be at peace and be content.

Later again I attended a conference. Someone had just given me about £25. I 'accidentally' met with another servant of the Lord, and we started talking. During our conversation I became aware that the Lord wanted me to give that brother the £25 I had just received. Somehow I understood that he needed it more than I did. So within the space of half an hour that sum of money changed hands again. The next day the Lord gave me back far more than I had given away. We have to learn this lesson over and over again: that we can call nothing our own, whether on the spiritual or the material level. We are quite simply stewards, and we are called to exercise wise stewardship with the things the Lord gives us. The Lord will never be any man's debtor either. We can never outgive Him for instance. In this way we learn to become more and more detached from money and earthly possessions. We begin to understand a little more and a little better each time that we are only pilgrims passing through this world.

For instance, it may be the Lord gives you or me a motorcar, and perhaps a month or a year later He may very well tell us to pass it on to another believer. In this way we also learn to be concerned and interested in the needs and necessities of others. A whole new area of service for Christ begins to open up of which the Lord Himself has said: 'It is more blessed to give than to receive' (Acts 20:35). You may perhaps not be able to go to far off lands to preach the gospel, or to take Bibles behind the Iron Curtain countries, or into the Arabic speaking world. Perhaps you are not even able to do anything very active in the Lord's service, but that does not deprive you at all from promoting and supporting the Lord's service and His servants by your intercession and giving.

Especially on the so-called missionfield it is not always easy to decide how much you should spend on buying or building a house and its furnishings, and what standard of living you are going to adopt. This is made even more difficult when we live and labour amongst people who live in deep poverty. It is absolutely essential for every servant of Christ to try to seek to integrate and become one with the people amongst whom he works. How far this integration is applied is a matter which cannot be measured by any general rule. It is a very personal matter in which the Lord leads and guides each individual servant. No case is the same. And we must remember that we can never satisfy everybody; even if we feel we have done everything we could, there will always be those who will criticize us.

I knew of a situation on the missionfield where a missionary family lived in a house in a small village where amazingly electricity was available, but they did not want to avail themselves of it. Every night the paraffin lamps were cleaned and lit. In this way they could still write home telling their fellow supporters of the primitive situation they lived in. It certainly gave quite a romantic touch to their lives and letters home. But let us not criticize. There is in each one of us a secret love for the heroic.

Those on the home-front should not prescribe the lifestyle of those who are in the front line on the mission-field. Let every man be fully persuaded in his own mind (Rom 14:5). We are all in danger at times of impressing others by letting them think how spiritual we are, and how sacrificial we are, and how ready we are to serve the Lord. Let us do these things as unto the Lord and not seek the praise of men, whether it be in the matter of giving materially, or serving others with the word of God. Let us do it in such a way that we do not draw any attention to ourselves.

Much tact, wisdom and sensitivity is needed in order to be able to give to others. How do we give? The one who receives, as well as the one who gives, both need much grace from the Lord. He who gives must do it in such a way that he will not hurt the feelings of him to whom he gives. The apostle Paul himself also was convinced of the delicacy of this ministry of giving. In Macedonia and Achaia the believers had gathered a substantial contribution for the poor believers at Jerusalem. Paul asks for prayer that this service of sharing materially with the believers at Jerusalem might be accepted of the saints there (Rom 15:31). Herein is a very important lesson for us. A lot of damage can be caused by a philanthropy without wisdom and tact. We are thinking particularly of giving for instance too much to someone, or to a project which does not really need all that it receives. The result of such indiscriminate giving is the creation of the so-called 'rice' Christians: people who become 'converts' simply for what they can get out of the servant of the Lord.

Experience

By experience I do not mean in this context being a handyman in practical crafts, but experiences in the life of faith. The question is often asked: 'Is it necessary for one to have had a lot of experience before one can serve the Lord?' There are of course a lot of different ways in which one can serve the Lord. But with the expression 'the performance of a service' in the New Testament is meant the use of a gift which a person has been given for a specific ministry.

To give a personal testimony is something we can all do for the Lord without being especially gifted or very experienced. We refer to the simple testimony of the man born blind in John 9:25: 'One thing I know, that, whereas I was blind, now I see'. Even someone who has only recently been born again can give a word of testimony which the Lord can use for His personal glory and the blessing of souls. The only experience we need for this is that we have had a personal encounter with the Lord and that we have come to know Him as our own personal Saviour. The keeper of the prison at Philippi immediately after his conversion did Paul and Silas a great service by showing them hospitality in his own home and binding up and caring for their wounds. He did not need any special gift for this service. There is a service for the Lord which is rendered in secret and which nevertheless is very precious and most blessed, and on the other hand there is service which is done in public and which is therefore seen by others.

A gift grows every time it is being experienced, and often without the person in question realising it. But the opposite is also true: if someone who has received a gift from the Lord does not use it, he will lose it. If I do not use or exercise my arm, it will dry up, and will finally become totally useless. This condition would be similar to someone who does not have an arm at all. A gift is therefore manifest by the use that is made of it. We will use it more and more, with much dedication. In this way a particular gift is discerned not only by ourselves but also by others.

It is not my purpose to write here of the many and various gifts. But it is a fact that in the function of the Body of Christ and her testimony in this world there is a great variety of gifts. There is a task to be done by every member of that Body, by every brother and sister. There is not a single believer who ever needs to say or think that for him or her there is nothing they can do for the Lord. It is also true that nobody is called upon to do anything for the Lord unless he or she is equipped and gifted for that particular service. If therefore a believer is trying to perform a service for which he or she is evidently not gifted, then that believer ought to ask himself very seriously whether he has really received a commission from the Lord, or whether he is doing it of his own choice.

The warning in Romans 12:3 is addressed to every one of us:' For I say, through the grace given unto me, to every man that is among you, not to think of himself more highly than he ought to think; but to think soberly, according as God hath dealt to every man the measure of faith'. Not only does the Lord through His Spirit grant a gift of grace to whom He will, but with that gift He also imparts a very personal and certain measure of faith which differs from one individual to another. This is the reason why the apostle Paul does not say 'as God hath dealt to ALL', but 'to EACH', personally and separately.

The spiritual level of believers is not the same in every case. One believer has more love and devotion for the Lord, and has given himself more willingly and un-reservedly to the Lord than another believer. We all differ in this respect. A more total surrender and devotion to the Lord will also result in an ever increasing measure of faith, and of spiritual energy and power in order to be able to use the particular gift. This process of ever increasing devotion to the Lord, and the daily growth in our love and affection for Him, is what I have in mind when I speak of experience in the context of this topic. This kind of experience is an absolute necessity for all believers, but especially for those contemplating service for the Lord. Dedication, or devotion of the heart to the Lord and His things, can commence the very moment a soul comes to know the Lord Jesus Christ as personal Saviour. There are for instance believers who may be very young in the faith, but who have grown up so quickly spiritually, that they possess more insight and discernment in spiritual things than others who have known the Lord perhaps for 10–15 years, and who are not spiritual but carnal Christians.

It is possible for someone to take up a service for the Lord for which he or she is not really fitted and which is far above their spiritual level and capacity. Not that they do not possess any gift at all for that particular service, but they lack spiritual power. That power is imparted as the result of an intimate life of fellowship and communion with the Lord. We have already discussed this earlier. Such a person therefore has need of a deepening and enriching of his spiritual experience before the gift which he has quite probably received will ripen into that maturity which the Lord has purposed.

Gifts in which the lack of spiritual power is most obvious to others are undoubtedly those of the evangelist, pastor and teacher. The gifts of pastor and teacher are exercised in the framework of the local assembly of believers for their edification. These gifts would therefore be judged and evaluated by all the believers present. By contrast, the gift of the evangelist is exercised in the world of unbelievers and is therefore discerned by all. When I say discerned, I mean that gifts or rather gifted persons are discerned or recognised and acknowledged by fellow believers as being indeed gifts of the Lord by

His Spirit and for which the believers can sincerely thank the Lord. The idea of a board or committee of men deciding whether a believer has a gift and appointing or ordaining such a gifted person to the service of the assembly is wholly foreign to the teaching of the New Testament.

If a believer (young or old) thinks that he possesses a gift from the Lord, then in the employment of that supposed gift it will become apparent if that particular believer has indeed truly received the gift and whether the measure of his faith and spiritual power (experience) is such that he is able to serve the Lord with His approval and blessing.

Experience is therefore something that is acquired in the secret life of faith of the believer. It is an ever increasing and overwhelming conviction of the truth and reality of the facts which one has accepted in faith, and which have now been tested and tried in the circumstances and happenings of every day life. Knowledge of the word of God is therefore absolutely essential before one would dare to serve others with that word, but it is not the only important factor. Spiritual power can only accompany our service if we have experienced personally the reality and actuality of God's word in the practice of our every day life.

In this respect time does play a role; in the case of one believer perhaps more than in the case of another believer. We gain experience when we have followed up the guidance and leading of the Lord in a particular matter, or in a problem which we had brought to Him in prayer. We gain experience by deliverances and answers to prayer which we have had or gone through in cases of danger or illness, difficult circumstances, sorrow and bereavement, loss and suffering. God uses all these in order to form us, to mature us and equip us so that we might become ever more increasingly a blessing to others and able to use our gifts for His glory.

The Lord Jesus first sent forth the twelve, and then the seventy to do His service, and in the doing of it they gained experience. Elijah gained tremendous experience when he prayed earnestly that it would not rain, and so it did not rain for three and a half years, and then; '...he prayed again, and the heaven gave rain, and the earth brought forth her fruit' (James 5:17, 18).

Faith must be exercised and tested so that it may be purified and strengthened and increased. The word 'experience' in the original text of the New Testament has the sense of proving (*peirazo/dokimazo*). When we have constructed a boat then we have to test it or prove its soundness by launching it into the water; only then shall we know its quality and whether any eventual alterations will be necessary. In the same way our faith is tested and tried, corrected and strengthened. The Samaritans will help us illustrate this point in what they say to the recently converted woman: 'Now we believe, not because of thy saying: for we have heard him ourselves, and know that this is indeed the Christ, the Saviour of the world' (Jn 4:42). Such experiences we can all gain everywhere, whether at home, or at school or college or university, at work, or in our contacts with others.

Finally let us consider the case of a believer who feels he is called to be an evangelist, whether at home or on the mission field. Suppose now that this brother is married. He feels that he has to give up his daily secular work in order to serve the Lord better. He would have to take into account the fact that it is utterly essential that his wife is willing to follow him in this new vocation. Have they both gained experience such as has been described above? Have they learned to look to the Lord alone in everything for their spiritual as well as their material support, and have they had actual experience of His provision? Have they experienced that the Lord does indeed hear and answer their prayers in practical ways? If they have not had such experiences before engaging full time in the Lord's service, and are contemplating giving up their secular work, it would be strongly recommended that they wait a little before taking such a step. No doubt the Lord will give to both of them complete and unshakable confirmation, in His time, that He has indeed called them to serve Him in this particular ministry. The matter would of course have to be even more seriously considered when the brother is not only married but also has a family.

In conclusion, we affirm that personal, spiritual experience is an absolute and essential element in the makeup of a call to serve the Lord in complete dependence upon Him, whether for spiritual or material necessities, and this principle applies to the unmarried as well as for the married and those who have families.

Practical qualities

In an American magazine, the 'Church Gazette', there once appeared the following advertisement:

'Urgently required: People with adaptability, who can mix concrete, and cross rivers, write articles, love their neighbours, can deliver babies, sit cross-legged for hours on end, conduct meetings, who are able to drain swamps, eat and digest all sorts of questionable dishes, have lots of patience with other humans, and suffer fools gladly, who are not afraid to dirty their hands or burn the midnight oil. Persons who are allergic to mosquitos and mice, babies and beggars, flies and filth, lice, indifference, itch, jungles, poverty and sweat, mildew and mud and unmarried mothers, had better think twice before applying'.

In connection with the above we would like to say a little about the different and various qualities which workers for the Lord should possess.

Adaptability

We can learn a tremendous amount in this respect from the apostle Paul, the greatest of all pioneer missionaries. He had many natural and practical qualities. Even if the Lord does not demand from us that we should be as 'all-round' as the apostle Paul, there are many things in which we may imitate him.

Many of us most probably possess some hidden talents which have to be awakened and cultivated. Often the circumstances in which we suddenly find ourselves may bring out those unrealised abilities. New situations present themselves and we have to adapt to new surroundings, people, perhaps even climates, languages and food. This is not so easy for some, but adaptability is an essential quality for those who desire to serve the Lord; otherwise they will feel cut off from the very people they seek to influence for Christ.

The apostle Paul was an intelligent man, but that was not the reason why the Lord chose him and called him to His service, although the Lord did use his intellectual capacities later. He had knowledge of Greek philosophy and poets, and even used this knowledge in his speech addressed to the people of Athens. He says of himself: 'I am made all things to all men, that I might by all means save some. And this I do for the gospel's sake...' (1 Cor 9:22, 23). He was of course a Jew by birth, but could speak fluent Greek and Aramaic; he had the privileges of a Roman citizen. These were no doubt, assets not to be despised but to be used for the Lord in His service.

In the life of a child of God nothing is insignificant and nothing is lost if only we lay it all in His hands. The apostle Paul had been brought up to adapt himself to all sorts of situations and to feel himself 'at home' anywhere. He was able to maintain a dialogue with the Hebrew theologians, as well as with pagan idolaters and very cultivated philosophers. He suited his words and speech to the mentality of his audience, and yet he could say: 'I came not with excellency of speech or of wisdom, declaring unto you the testimony of God' (1 Cor 2:1). His speeches to the civil authorities testify of a clear insight and thorough knowledge of their character, customs and cultures. He was able to adapt himself effortlessly in his service to all sorts of people: counsellors, soldiers, sailors, kings, governors, Roman civil servants, men and women.

It is particularly those who feel the Lord is calling them to service abroad who must be convinced of the absolute necessity of acquainting themselves thoroughly with the history, culture, behaviour pattern, and people of the land to which they feel they might be called to serve. It is difficult to imagine that the Lord would call anyone to serve in a country, or a situation, in which the person concerned is totally disinterested, or of which he is totally ignorant.

A very interesting source of information is available to all who would but correspond with those who are in active service for the Lord either at home or on the missionfield. How encouraging it is also for those who serve the Lord in lonely outposts on the missionfield, when they receive letters from those at home. 'As cold waters to a thirsty soul, so is good news from a far country' (Prov 25:25). We should all take a deep interest in missionary work and share with our missionary brothers and sisters by daily praying for them. But we cannot pray intelligently for them if we do not know their needs and circumstances.

For those who are really interested, there are the magazines and papers of missionary activities, biographies of William Carey, Hudson Taylor, C. T. Studd, Mary Slessor, David Livingstone and many other modern and contemporary missionary biographies, which can be read with very great profit and blessing and which will widen our horizon. Why is it that such literature is so little read among believers today? It is no wonder that many believers are almost totally ignorant of the vast world-wide work of evangelism and the Lord's service abroad. Are we then completely devoid of interest and indifferent to the fact that there are still today millions of souls in this sad world who have never yet heard the gospel of our Lord Jesus Christ? Brothers and sisters, who read these lines, have you ever won a soul for Christ? Do you want others to come to know your Saviour? What are you doing about it?

There are so many who are actively spreading false teachings and establishing false and antichristian cults. How shall men and women hear the pure truth if we do not take it to them? Those whom the Lord Jesus is calling to lands where non-Christian religions dominate, will need to acquaint themselves thoroughly with these false teachings so that they can understand the reasoning and religious background of those they seek to win for Christ, and be able to convince their hearers with the word of God. It is of course quite clear that we do not at all recommend all believers indiscriminately to study heresies, as they do not need this knowledge, which could be positively harmful to them.

Perseverance

Determination and resoluteness are also essential elements in the believer's armour (Eph 6:13). How many there are who start something and never finish it! The Lord Jesus spoke of such in His parable in Luke 14:25–33, where He tells of someone who wants to build a tower, and of a king who wants to make war with another king, and who do not first sit down to calculate the cost of such expensive ventures, to see whether they will be able to accomplish their exploits or not. Determination to finish that which one has begun demands a tremendous amount of self-discipline and help of the Holy Spirit. This principle holds true for all God's children, but particularly for those who are privileged to do a little service for the Lord, whether in their own country or abroad.

To have to do the same thing day after day creates in many the desire to do something different, to go somewhere else. We all think sometimes that the grass is greener on the other side of the fence. We are dissatisfied, unfulfilled. We think that if only we could get away from our present situation, and if only we could be somewhere else or in another country even, things would be much easier and happier, and we are convinced that there we could serve the Lord much more effectively. In this way the enemy often succeeds in sowing unrest in our hearts, and we are thus disqualified and useless for doing anything at all. We must be honest with ourselves, and willing to recognise our handicaps and limitations, in prayer before the Lord. But this does not mean that we ought to be inactive, or give up, but in spite of what is apparently lacking in our make-up, we should cast ourselves on the Lord and seek to do the things close at hand with His help.

How many things there were in the apostle Paul's life which might have discouraged him completely! He himself tells us of a few: '...in labours more abundant, in stripes above measure, in prisons more frequent, in death oft. Of the Jews five times received I forty stripes save one. Thrice was I beaten with rods, once was I stoned, thrice I suffered shipwreck, a night and a day I have been in the deep; in journeyings often, in perils of waters, in perils of robbers, in perils by mine own countrymen, in perils by the heathen, in perils in the city, in perils in the wilderness, in perils in the sea, in perils among false brethren; in weariness and painfulness, in watchings often, in hunger and thirst, in fastings often, in cold and nakedness. Beside those things that are without, that which cometh upon me daily, the care of all the churches. Who is weak, and I am not weak?

who is offended, and I burn not?' 'We are fools for
Christ' sake, but ye are wise in Christ; we are weak, but
ye are strong; ye are honourable, but we are despised.
Even unto this present hour we both hunger, and thirst,
and are naked, and are buffeted, and have no certain
dwelling-place; and labour, working with our hands:
being reviled, we bless; being persecuted, we suffer it:
being defamed, we intreat: we are made as the filth of
the world, and are the offscouring of all things unto this
day' (2 Cor 11:23–29; 1 Cor 4:10–13).

Is there someone reading this who is thoroughly discouraged? Brothers, sisters, you who serve the Lord
whether at home or abroad, perhaps somewhere lonely
and deserted, are you asking yourself at this moment
whether it is worth it to go on with what you are doing?
Just think of Paul the apostle. He saw so many of his
friends and fellow-labourers and fellow believers desert-
ing him (2 Tim 1:15; 4:10). He met with indifference
from his own fellow-believers. Not just indifference, but
also deadly opposition, criticism and slander! But he did
not give up. He strengthened himself in the Lord, as
David did, and persevered. Let us all take strength from
the Lord to continue where we are and in what we are
doing for Him, in dependence upon Him. He will never
let us down. The question is really whether we will let
Him down.

Obedience

'Have not I commanded thee? Be strong and of a good
courage; be not afraid, neither be thou dismayed; for the
Lord thy God is with thee whithersoever thou goest'
(Josh 1:9). Imagine that you have come to a decision.
You have quietly considered every angle, and you have
laid it in prayer before the Lord; you have asked for His
guidance, you are sure that this must be His will for you.
Well then, now the decisive moment has come, do not
fear or hesitate, but step out in faith. Trust the Lord to

show you the next step and the next. Be willing for correction: if He shuts this door, He may open one in another direction. Of course there will be difficulties, and opposition, and even dangers. But we must look up to our God, and not see the giants, and so join with Caleb and Joshua, who said: 'Let us go up at once, and possess it; for we are well able to overcome it' (Num 13:30).

We often suffer most from what we fear might happen to us. There is however a very thin line between a fanatical stubborn attitude, and what we might call the obedience of faith: happy the one who can discern the difference and avoid the former! Cowardly and fearful believers know nothing of the strength and fortitude of faith that is a result of the presence of the Lord when we dare to set one foot in the path of the impossible and there find a foothold and a path which He opens up. Courage means that we perceive the task which God has given us to do, and that we want to do it, certain of His presence, confident of His promises, discovering His power as we obey His every word and command. This kind of courage is a gift from God, just as much as faith is; it is not found naturally in ourselves.

I sat in my room in our office of the Watch- and Jewellers' Headquarters in The Hague. That morning I had received a prospectus of a missionary training college in the north of England. In 1949 the sum of £25 represented quite a fortune for a young man like myself, but that was the fee for one term at college. I did not possess that much money, although I earned more than most of my friends. Rather disappointed I pulled out of my brief-case a book entitled 'The Work God blesses', written by Oswald Smith of Toronto. Quite 'accidentally' it fell open somewhere in the middle, and my eyes caught the following line at the bottom of the page: 'One day we needed a large sum of money for the work of the Lord which we did not possess. We laid this need before the

Lord in prayer, and He wonderfully answered our prayers by giving us even more than we asked for'. Had I read this properly? Do such miracles still happen today? Much impressed by what I had just read, I took my Bible and asked the Lord to speak to me through it. I turned to the book of Joshua and began to read at chapter one, v.1. Then I came to v.9, and read: 'Have not I commanded thee? ...'. It was just as if the Lord Jesus Himself stood there in my little room and said to me: 'You can trust Me. I will take care of you, and will go with you'. From the depth of my heart I responded with: 'Yes. Lord I believe. I will go'.

Some time later an elderly sister in Christ rang me up at my office. I did not know her personally, and she had only heard about me through others. She had a children's home somewhere in Holland. She told me that she wanted to see me, as she had an important message for me. Please would I come to see her as soon as possible? Seated in her living room she said to me: 'One morning this week I was praying, and then it seemed as if the Lord asked me a question. "To whom do you belong?" I said, "I belong to you, dear Lord". "And what about your home?" "That also belongs to you, dear Lord". "But what about your bank-account?" "All the money I possess is yours, dear Lord". "Very well then," said the Lord, "take an envelope and put in so many guilders and give it to Cor Bruins".' Then she handed me the envelope and told me not to open it until I had arrived home. Once home, I called my parents to listen to this incredible story, and then I opened the envelope. Can you imagine our astonishment when out came the equivalent of £50. I had never seen so much money!

How wonderful of the Lord to have told this child of His to act in this way, and how pleased the Lord must have been that she obeyed without asking questions. After all, she did not even know me personally; she had heard from others that I had this desire to serve the

Lord. Obedience always results in blessing. This was the first miracle I had ever personally experienced. It was also the first of an unending chain of miracles of God's wondrous care and provision that has never ceased up till this very moment as I write these lines. Yes, a thousand times, He is the God of the impossible! Yes, even today He hears and answers prayer! Yes, His arm is not shortened that it cannot do miracles today!

You will appreciate that all this was a tremendous encouragement to me to continue with the Lord in the pathway. He knew all that still lay ahead in this pilgrim pathway of the life of faith. So I left for College, paid the fees for the first term, bought books and many other necessary items, and worked out the balance of the cash remaining. It was by no means enough for the second term. During that first term I became close friends with Dennis. We used to rise early in the morning to pray for one another and many other needs. About ten weeks of term had passed and still I had not a penny towards my fees for the second term. The enemy often told me that I should return home as it was obvious that the Lord was not with me. One morning when Dennis and I were praying, Dennis suddenly stopped in the middle of his prayer. I said 'What is the matter?' 'Well', he said, 'the Lord seems to say to me, "Dennis, you are asking me to provide for your brother. Be practical, you have money in your bank-account. I want to use that bank-account to pay for your brother's fees".' So Dennis shared with me, and paid for me right through College. What endless blessing resulted for me personally from that act of obedience of my pal. This book would become too big if I told you all the many miracles the Lord wrought for me personally during the next five years or so that I studied in England.

'Be of good courage...' said our text. And we need to be reminded of this daily. We will meet with difficulties, needs, deprivations, opposition and criticism from fellow-believers and others. We have a proverb in Dutch which says: 'Tall trees catch a lot of wind', meaning, that if you are in the front line of the spiritual battle, you are going to be much exposed to attack from the enemy, and this may come through friend as well as foe. Those who are active for the Lord will have to put up with a lot more criticism than those who do nothing. Criticism very often comes from the comfortable armchair Christians. When you are inactive you cannot make a lot of mistakes. Romans 12:17–21 is important to remember when you feel that you have been unjustly criticised or perhaps even slandered. Someone said: 'To reward good with good is human; to recompense evil for good is devilish; to reward evil for evil is bestial. But to recompense good for evil, that is what God does!'

Common sense

When we were still in our sinful condition as natural men, unregenerate, our hearts (or our intellects) were also unenlightened and darkened (Rom 12:1). But now that we have been born again, the Holy Spirit works in us to transform us by renewing our mind (Rom 12:2; 1 Cor 2:16). A believer who has surrendered his spirit and soul and body to the Lord, to obey Him, and who maintains this attitude of yieldedness daily, is now enabled to use his sound and sanctified mind to discern God's will and to do it.

A true believer who sincerely loves the Lord has the desire to do His will, and not his own. He will look for every available opportunity to glorify his Lord and Master. The apostle Paul also used his common sense. His 'self-will' had been crucified with Christ on the cross. His will and desires were now in harmony with the will of God. God does not make automatons of His children, or programmed computers! God's Spirit LEADS the believer. He never drives them in front of Him like a herd of dumb cattle. That is the method of Satan. He has slaves whom he bullies and drives and compels to do his will. God's spirit will always seek the reasonable, intelligent and voluntary cooperation of the believer.

We believe that the apostle Paul also prayerfully made his plans. He also had intentions. There is nothing wrong in this. It is not wrong for us to make plans either. But of course it is quite wrong to make our own plans first and decide what we are going to do, and then to go to the Lord and ask for His approval! This is not the way in which we should use our sanctified common sense. Doing everything with Him and in dependence upon Him, that is what the Lord expects from us.

Strategy

The apostle Paul was a missionary strategist. He gave much careful thought to his personal life-style, a life of faith, in his service for Christ. He gives his personal testimony concerning this fact: 'I therefore so run, not as uncertainly; so fight I, not as one that beateth the air.' (1 Cor 9:26). No doubt it would do us all a great deal of good to read this whole ninth chapter of 1st Corinthians again. In Romans 15:19–21 Paul describes his strategy as follows: '...so that from Jerusalem, and round about unto Illyricum, I have fully preached the gospel of Christ ...not where Christ was named, lest I should build upon another man's foundation' (see also the rest of the chapter.)

He went from place to place evangelising. As soon as there were converts, he would teach them: '...how I kept back nothing that was profitable unto you, but have shewed you, and have taught you publicly, and from house to house... for I have not shunned to declare unto you all the counsel of God' (Acts 20:20, 27). When the believers in a certain place were established in the truth, he sometimes then looked for capable and responsible men in those localities who could teach the believers (2 Tim 2:1, 2), but he himself would continue to evangelise in the regions beyond.

We are all agreed, no doubt, that this is scriptural strategy. In our day of fervent nationalism on the so-called missionfields, it is of the utmost importance that we take good notice of this movement. Those who serve the Lord in the gospel in foreign lands, especially in the third world, are not only considered to be foreigners (no matter how hard they try to integrate), but are often suspected of being imperialists, spies and colonialists. When such situations are prevalent, the best strategy to follow is still the age-old strategy of Paul.

As soon as a born again nucleus of national believers is formed, and as soon as there are believers who are established and versed in the truth, the evangelist ought to commit them to the care of the Holy Spirit and the Word of God. If this strategy is not successful, then the servant of the Lord ought to examine himself as to what the reason for this might be. Paul writes in 1 Thessalonians 1:5, 6: 'For our gospel came not unto you in word only, but also in power, and in the Holy Ghost, and in much assurance; as ye know what manner of men we were among you for your sake. And ye became followers of us, and of the Lord, having received the word in much affliction...' The Spirit of God may be hindered by us. Perhaps we think that our way of doing things, our own strategy, is the best, and we are not open for the Spirit's leading. We may substitute traditionalism, or human logic, for the Spirit's leading, and the result is fruitlessness.

Another important aspect of missionary strategy is the necessity for after care. In the medical world we call it postnatal care. Spiritual babes and growing children need help and assistance. See what Paul feels about this in Acts 15:36. 'And some days after, Paul said unto Barnabas, Let us go again and visit our brethren in every city where we have preached the word of the Lord, and see how they do'. There is a great need for encouraging one another in the Lord, to care for believers who perhaps never, or very seldom, have visitors, and who feel lonely and isolated. This need exists everywhere, and we ought to pray the Lord to give us more believers with a shepherd heart who care for the sheep and help them grow in the Lord.

No doubt, in selecting his fellow-workers the apostle Paul also used his pure sanctified mind and spiritual insight under the direction of the Holy Spirit. In Acts 15:36–41 we see for instance that for certain definite reasons he did not feel that John Mark should accompany him on his second missionary journey. But later on, we see how Paul could praise this same young man, and appreciated his usefulness in the Lord's service. (2 Tim 4:11).

Paul and Barnabas were both called by the Lord Jesus to serve Him, even to serve Him together. But there came a moment in their missionary career that they separated from each other. Although expositors of the scriptures have tried to side with Paul against Barnabas, we ought to be very careful in drawing conclusions. It is a remarkable fact, however, that from the moment Barnabas separated himself from Paul we do not hear of him again.

Apollos also was a servant of Christ who felt his personal responsibility to the Lord very strongly. We may well accept that the reason why he would not accept Paul's urging him to visit Corinth was because of his deep affection and respect for Paul, and not necessarily a difference of opinion (as if he might have said: 'Let the saints at Corinth first of all determine their proper attitude towards brother Paul, then I might consider the invitation'.). But Paul did respect Apollos' decision not to go (1 Cor 16:12).

It may still happen today that two respected servants of Christ do not see eye to eye in everything. But they ought to have sufficient love for one another that they mutually respect each other. In other words, they agree to differ. There is nothing wrong in that. You can live in peace with someone with whom you do not necessarily see eye to eye. Sometimes Abraham's example may have to be followed, as described in Genesis 13:8,9 where we read: 'Let there be no strife, I pray thee, between me and thee,...for we be brethren...separate thyself, I pray thee, from me: if thou wilt take the left hand, then I will go to the right; or if thou depart to the right hand, then I will go to the left.' It is ultimately better to separate with mutual respect for one another and not to serve the Lord in the same place rather than to remain and because of constant bickering break down that which is set up with so much effort.

It would be very profitable for each one desiring to serve the Lord to make a thorough study of the Acts of the Apostles. The book should really be called 'The Acts of the Holy Spirit', or for our purpose: 'The strategy and method of the Holy Spirit'. There we will find an excellent pattern and guide-line for evangelisation, missionary activity, and building up of assemblies. In this book of missionary strategy we see how Paul directs his offensive more and more towards the big cities and metropoli, knowing that from these centres the greatest influence will be exerted upon the culture and habits of the population.

He aimed his gospel at the influential people as well as at the under-privileged. He always did his utmost to further the growth and harmony of the assembly. He did not consider his evangelistic ministry as an aim in itself, but he did, however, see it is an activity of utmost necessity and indispensable to the eventual establishment of local assemblies which should become indigenous as soon as possible, and thus be able to maintain themselves spiritually as well as materially. The amount of time he gave to this was not bound by hard and fast rules. In Thessalonica, for instance, it seems that he could only stay for about one month with those young converts (c.f. Acts 17:2 'three sabbath days'). In Corinth and Ephesus he remained much longer. He had tremendous insight and spiritual discernment as to whom he could trust with responsibilities and authority, which he considered a very important and essential matter in the establishing of the believers everywhere.

Preaching

The method the apostle Paul adopted in presenting the word of God often depended upon the circumstances. This is a very important point to consider for all who desire to serve the Lord, and minister His word. There are believers who are unable to express themselves in a way in which they might have been able to had they received a better education, but nevertheless their simple words touch the heart because of their truthfulness. God has His servants in educated and intellectual circles, just as much as in the slums, and amongst the head-hunters, and Auca Indians. For each of these groups, or sections of mankind, God has His instruments prepared by the Holy Spirit to be able to work amongst these particular people. Now, there is no need at all for there to be jealousy, or even criticism between those who have received a particular ministry from the Lord. Every one of them is simply required to do his utmost with the talents he has received of the Lord of the harvestfield.

Sometimes Paul's preaching was polemical: that is to say that it had the character of a controversy (read for instance Acts 9:22: 'But Saul increased the more in strength, and confounded the Jews which dwelt at Damascus, proving that this is very Christ'.). They were unable to gainsay Paul's logic. He was a clear thinker who had prayerfully come to strong convictions in his own mind, and who was therefore able to refute all possible kinds of arguments. When he was in Athens, we read in Acts 17:17: 'Therefore disputed he in the synagogue with the Jews, and with the devout persons, and in the market daily with them that met with him'. At Corinth: '…he reasoned in the synagogue every sabbath, and persuaded the Jews and the Greeks' (Acts 18:4). But he did not fall into the trap of engaging in discussions simply to win the argument. We can sometimes win an argument, and lose a precious soul.

At other times Paul's preaching might be persuasive, with abundant pleading. He did not only give the facts and arguments, as if these were sufficient, but: 'knowing therefore the terror of the Lord, we persuade men', was his motto (see 2 Cor 5:11). Again, Paul might adopt the didactical method of preaching, which simply means that it had the character of a lecture. He continued two years teaching daily in the school of Tyrannus (Acts 19:9).

We must never presume that we can do the work of the Holy Spirit, even though we might be able to speak with tremendous earnestness. The other day someone said to me, whilst discussing speakers in general, that for him the golden rule was: 'Stand up, speak up, shut up'. We may smile about this, or we may say that nobody should try to prescribe to the Holy Spirit how He ought to direct a speaker. But I believe that it is of the utmost importance how we speak, and what we say, and when. In Proverbs 25:11 we read these challenging words: 'A word fitly spoken is like apples of gold in pictures of silver'.

Some speakers read the scriptures very carelessly, without commas, rests, intonation, or modulation. In short, it sounds terribly monotonous and utterly boring. To read in such a fashion is definitely not a manifestation of piety or spirituality. '…the word of God is quick, and powerful, and sharper than any twoedged sword….', we read in Hebrews 4:12. The reading aloud in public of the word of God is in itself already a most powerful kind of preaching. Whatever the preacher is going to add to that in his exposition is definitely not the most important. That is why it is of the utmost importance that the one who reads God's word in public does so in a clear and distinct manner, so that the hearts of his hearers may be touched, and as it were prepared. Unfortunately however, many hearers lose interest during the monotonous reading of the scriptures, and are switched off before the reading is over. They will take home very little of value for their spiritual lives.

How different it was in the days of Nehemiah, for we read in his book: '...Ezra the scribe stood upon a pulpit of wood, which they had made for the purpose...and Ezra opened the book in the sight of all the people, (for he was above all the people;)...they read in the book in the law of God distinctly, and gave the sense, and caused them to understand the reading.' (8:4–6). We are told here even how Ezra stood in order to read; apparently this is important enough for the Holy Spirit to bring it to our attention. We may well ask how the speaker today stands in front of his hearers. Is there anything particularly noticeable about his dress, hair, appearance that would divert the attention of the hearers from the Lord, and rather fix the attention on himself?

Another thing the Holy Spirit tells us is the manner in which Ezra opened the book. This again seems to be of importance. It can manifest to the hearer the deep respect the reader has for the book he reads from. This is something that ought always to be obvious to the hearers; the reverence and respect the reader has for the word of God. It is for this reason that he should always endeavour to read it prayerfully, and as distinctly and clearly as possible with the help of the Holy Spirit. Did you know that the Muslims would never put their Koran on the floor? They would never dare to put any other object on top of the Koran, their holy book. A Muslim would never place the Koran beside his feet. In fact he handles the Koran with utmost respect. You just could not imagine for instance a Muslim reading Koran in public with his hand(s) in his pocket(s).

And last but not least, we read in Nehemiah chapter 8 that not only was the word of God read distinctly, but that it was furthermore so explained and commented upon that every one present understood. Some speakers are so confusing in their utterances, jumping about from one subject to another, that the hearers cannot distinguish head from tail! Not only do they not remain within the framework of the subject they announced they would speak on, but in a veritable flood of words and an unending stream of texts and references, they go from north to south, and from east to west. No wonder that after a short time having listened to such a speaker most of his audience have lost interest, or have even gone to sleep! Such speakers feel that now the moment has come to rouse those sleepy heads by raising their voices and beating hard with their fists on the pulpit. You can well imagine how little spiritual profit there is from such ministry.

In conclusion, the speaker ought to have enough control over his own spirit to know when to stop. We will not say any more about this subject, but simply refer the reader to what Paul says in 1 Corinthians 14:32 'And the spirits of the prophets are subject to the prophets'.

Linguistics abilities

This topic is really only addressed to those of my readers who think the Lord may be calling them to service in foreign countries. There are people who have a natural aptitude and gift for learning foreign languages. Others find language great tongue-twisters. By the time a young person is about 18 years of age, there need no longer be any doubt whether one has or has not a gift for languages.

We have already remarked earlier that a believer should use his sanctified common sense, and that it is best for him to remain within the limits of the measure of his faith and the particular gift he has received of the Lord. We believe it is true to say that the Lord would not normally call any one to a task or a service for which he has absolutely no ability (read Matt 25:15).

Paul writes to tbe believers at Corinth in his first letter chapter seven, that if a bachelor wants to get married, he does not sin if he marries. But Paul would try to dissuade him because of the peculiarly difficult circumstances of those days of widespread persecution and danger. Paul wants to spare him extra sufferings. It is with this same purpose in view that we add this topic of languages. Someone who has not been born with a natural gift for languages does much better not to seek to serve the Lord in a foreign country, if the Lord does not direct him or her that way. He would save himself many tears.

For someone who serves the Lord in his home-country ignorance of foreign languages is not any obstacle. But someone who believes the Lord is calling him to a foreign country, and who has no gift for languages, and nevertheless pursues that way is going to have a very, very hard time. We have known friends who served the Lord in the Arabic speaking world. I am thinking in particular of a doctor in biology who for years tried to master the Arabic language. But he never managed to get past the stage where he did not need an interpreter. This was indeed a daily, recurring, unbearable burden and sorrow for this brother in Christ. He was not able to have personal contact with the people of the country where he served, and so could never enter into, or share, their problems. One could wonder whether the Lord had called this dear man to serve Him in that country. We can all make mistakes as to guidance.

The learning of the current language (or sometimes more than one) is of utmost importance, and should have absolute priority on the daily work-program of a newly arrived worker. Of course we do not mean that because someone has difficulty learning a foreign language he is therefore unfit for the Lord's service abroad, or that he cannot be a blessing. We just feel we should give a little word of advice here. It may be this could be of help to someone and avoid disappointments.

It is possible, whilst at home, to test ourselves as to whether we could handle languages. There are many language courses one can follow privately. To begin with, it would be very useful thoroughly to master the grammar of one's own language! Languages are taught at school much more today than 30 years ago! Many young people with a desire to serve the Lord often try to get a job in a foreign country, or they follow special language courses given at different European Universities during the summer holidays. Others have benefited from courses in linguistics, and work and study with the Wycliffe Bible translators for instance.

Knowledge of a language is useful. But no one ought to think that because he knows a foreign language he must therefore serve the Lord in that particular foreign language he happens to have learned. This is something the Lord will make abundantly clear in His own good time. However, all practical knowledge is a tremendous asset, and useful for a child of God. It all depends where the Lord wants us to serve Him, whether we shall be able to put whatever abilities we have into practice. For those who are ready to serve the Lord when He calls them, it is advisable that they gear their preparations or studies in that direction.

There seems to be an idea amongst many uninformed believers that missionary work abroad consists purely in preaching and teaching the word of God. This is however far from reality. One who loves the Lord, but has not received the gift of an evangelist, or pastor or teacher, is nevertheless very much needed in many areas today where primitive conditions still exist and prevail. Most professions are still needed on many missionfields. Believers who are knowledgeable about mechanics, motor cars, planes, electronics, generators, hygiene, bricklaying, carpentry, shoe-repair, who have know-ledge of tropical diseases and medicine, midwives, nurses, doctors, cooks and tailors, architects, typists, administrators and bookkeepers, agricultural and civil engineers, printers and photographers, and many other crafts, are at a premium on many a mission-field. There is a crying need for dedicated Christians who are willing to do an ordinary job for the Lord.

Will you not lay your all in his hands, and say: 'Here am I, Lord, send me.'?

PART THREE

THE PERSON IN QUESTION – YOU!

7

GOD IS CALLING *YOU*

We have now arrived at the third part of our text upon which the contents of this book are based. You remember how we divided that verse in John 20:21 – Part One: Christ our Pattern, 'As the Father has sent me ...' Part Two: The Preparation, 'So send I ...' Part Three: The Person, '... You ...'

In the first part of the book we saw how the Lord Jesus was sent by the Father, and that the Lord Himself also sends forth His followers into this world. The mission of the disciples takes its character from the way in which the Lord Jesus was sent by His Father. He is therefore our Pattern and Example. But before the Lord sends forth His own, He wants them to be with Him and learn from Him (Matt 11:29; Mark 3:14).

In the second part we have seen how each disciple of the Lord Jesus has his or her place in 'the school of God', where the subject taught is Jesus Christ Himself, and where the Holy Spirit is the Teacher. Although disciples of Jesus Christ never finish studying and learning, there comes a moment in their lives when they realise that what they have learned must now be put into practice. It may be that a believer has not realised that he or she is indeed a pupil enrolled in the school of God. But whether he realises it or not does not change the fact, because it happened the moment he was born again.

So then, we can be either consciously or unconsciously pupils in the school of God, willing or unwilling students. That moment when we realise that we are actually in that school, and that the Lord asks from us all that we submit ourselves to the direction and teaching of His Spirit, is the subject we want to deal with in this third and last part of the book. Here then we have come to the decisive moment for each one of us. The question does not only concern just a few very gifted believers who have received a specific call from the Lord to a specific ministry, but we are talking here about the call to discipleship addressed to *all* believers.

The most important thing for a believer is not what he or she does for Christ, but whether we have consciously and willingly submitted ourselves to the Lord in complete surrender. This is the reason why the title of this third part of the book is so intensely personal. The focus is on *you* and *me*. Yes, *you* also. Not those other brothers and sisters in Christ, not those only who have received a specific service from the Lord, but you and me, ordinary believers. Yes, my dear brother and sister, the Lord is calling you. Have you realised that He has been calling you ever since you came to know Him as your personal Saviour, so that you might follow Him as His disciple?

He does not call us in the first place in order that we might become missionaries abroad. He does not call us in the first place that we might serve Him, but that we might *follow* Him, and live for Him, by letting Him live in and through us, just there where He has placed us. So then, should we not all become missionaries? Perhaps! How can you be sure about that? Let us begin by asking what in fact is meant by being a missionary?

'A missionary' – what's that?

A missionary quite simply is someone who is sent on behalf of another: 'Now then we are ambassadors for Christ...' (2 Cor 5:20). The fundamental point for us to remember is that it is not so important, in the first instance, what he who has been sent does, or where he has been sent, but whether he or she is totally submitted and committed to the One Who sent them – Christ. All born again believers without exception ought to be characterised by this willing spirit. This willingness is part and parcel of our personal capitulation to Jesus Christ. It includes the surrender of our own ego. The word missionary therefore is not exclusively the title of a brother or sister who serves the Lord in Zaire, Egypt, the Cameroon or Colombia.

The realisation of being sent can be the experience of all those who want to live for the Lord, whether they are mothers with their children at home, nurses in hospital, typists and secretaries in the office, sales men and women, directors or managers or teachers, with or without profession, married or unmarried, intellectual or ordinary, gifted or not gifted. There is no believer, no member in the Body of Christ, who is not included in this personal call of the Lord Jesus Christ to follow Him wherever He may lead. We have all without exception, been called to be witnesses and light-bearers for Him in this dark world: '...and ye shall be witnesses unto me ...(Acts 1:8), 'that ye may be blameless and harmless, the sons of God, without rebuke, in the midst of a crooked and perverse nation, among whom ye shine as lights in the world.' (Phil 2:15).

In Luke 9, we see the Lord Jesus on the way to Jerusalem (v.51), which ultimately led Him to the cross of Calvary. 'And it came to pass, that, as they went in the way, a certain man said unto Him, Lord, I will follow thee whithersoever thou goest' (v.57). How wonderful to see this man so full of enthusiasm wanting to follow the Lord! And yet it seems as if the Lord dampens this enthusiasm in the answer He gives: 'Foxes have holes, and birds of the air have nests; but the Son of man hath not where to lay his head' (v.58). Did the Lord not want this person to follow Him after all? Certainly, but the Lord wanted to test the sincerity of his enthusiasm. Had this man really seriously thought about what it would mean to follow Jesus Christ...whithersoever He went? It is possible for us all, in a moment when our emotions are deeply stirred, to promise something without having asked ourselves seriously and realistically what it will entail.

The Lord Jesus never hides from us what it costs to follow Him as His disciples. Hear what He says in Luke 9:23 'If any man will come after me, let him deny himself, and take up his cross daily, and follow me.' 'If any man come to me, and hate not his father, and mother, and wife, and children, and brethren, and sisters, yea, and his own life also, he cannot be my disciple. And whoso-ever doth not bear his cross, and come after me, cannot be my disciple. For which of you, intending to build a tower, sitteth not down first, and counteth the cost, whether he have sufficient to finish it' (Luke 14:26–28).

Often we hear the Lord say: 'Come, follow me' (i.e. Matt 4:19; 8:22; 9:9; 16:24; 19:21; Mark 2:14; 8:34; 10:21; Luke 5:27; 9:23,59; 18:22; John 1:43; 12:26; 21:22 etc). Sometimes we also read of people who followed the Lord as a result of having had a personal encounter with Him: Matthew 4:20,22; 9:27; Mark 1:18; Luke 5:11,28. He is still calling us all today. What will be your and my response?

The great commission

Please will you first look up the following references? Matthew 28:16–20; Mark 16:15–20; Luke 24:36–49; John 20:19–23. These verses describe what is generally called 'The Great Commission'. In this Great Commission we will find the basis for the call of Christ, and we shall discover also to whom this call is addressed.

To whom is it addressed?

a. In Matthew (28:16–20) this commission is exclusively addressed to the eleven apostles, the symbolic faithful remnant of the nation of Israel. As Israelites they have yet to accomplish their great worldwide task.

b. In Mark (16:15–20) the commission seems to be given also to the eleven. This evangelist gives very few details.

c. In Luke (24:36–49) we see the eleven apostles in the foreground, but others are also mentioned: '...that were with them.' (verse 33).

d. In John (20:19–23) we have no specific commission; only Peter and John are addressed by the Lord concerning a ministry which they had to do for the Lord. Here we have neither a mountain mentioned, nor Galilee, nor Bethany, as in the Synoptic gospels.

What must they do?

a. In Matthew they are simply told: 'Go ye therefore...' (v.19).

b. In Mark they receive a similar command (v.15).

c. In Luke they are told to remain in Jerusalem, until they are endued with power from on high (v.49; Acts 1:8). The Lord does not say that they all have to be evangelists, because this special gift is not given to everyone, but all must be witnesses.

d. In John we do not read that the disciples are sent forth from Jerusalem. The Lord Himself says to them: 'Even so send I you...(v.21). Neither Jerusalem, nor any other specific place is mentioned.

What is the message they must preach?

a. In Matthew we clearly distinguish the background of the typical character of this Gospel which has especially the coming King and His kingdom in view. The Messiah will come to reign as King – He who at first was rejected, but who after His second coming in glory will reign a thousand years. To Him everything and everybody must be submitted. By way of preparation the apostles are sent forth to: 1) make disciples, 2) to baptize, and 3) to teach them to observe what the King had taught His disciples in the sermon on the mount (chapters 5, 6, 7). The preaching of the gospel of *grace* is not mentioned here, neither the message that all men must repent – a fact which no doubt is included, or assumed, although it is not specifically mentioned.

b. In Mark we are told very clearly that the gospel, which means 'good news', must be preached (v.15).

c. In Luke we see that connected with the preaching of the good news of salvation through the sacrifice of Christ, also repentance and forgiveness must be preached (v.47). In fact, it is this gospel which we find clearly described as being the theme of our present day preaching.

d. In John we do not see the apostles as such, but rather the disciples. In other words, believers without distinction (v.19). To all of them is said that their message is to be a message of peace (v.21).

To whom must this message be taken?

a. According to Matthew's Gospel the message is now no longer exclusively directed to the limited circle of Judaism (10:6; 15:24), but it has become a worldwide message to all nations (28:19).

b. Mark's Gospel tell us that the preaching is also to be taken into all the world and to every creature (16:15).

c. In Luke we read that the message must be taken to all nations (24:47).

d. Our Lord Jesus says in John's Gospel: '...even so have I also sent them into the world. (17:18). Here again we have the world-wide scope of the preaching emphasized.

In whose power must the preaching be done?

It must be done in the power which the Holy Spirit imparts. Luke in his Gospel emphasizes this very clearly; the disciples must first be clothed and filled with power from on high (v.49). In Matthew and Mark, the Holy Spirit is not mentioned in this connection.

Signs and wonders

Only Mark says: '...these signs shall follow...(v.17). From Hebrews 2:4 we know that this indeed has taken place. Those who after the founding of the Church on earth went forth preaching the Gospel, received as a confirmation from God that they had been sent by Him, a special seal from God: they had the ability given them to do signs and wonders and many miracles according as the Holy Spirit led them. It was at the same time an indication that a new era, or period in God's economy had begun: that of the Church and the Holy Spirit's indwelling in the believers.

In Luke's Gospel we read nothing about signs and wonders following, nor about baptism, nor yet about the making of disciples and teaching them what the Lord had commanded. We can see quite clearly that the commission here has a totally different character from that described in the gospel of Matthew and Mark.

In John's Gospel we read about the remitting of sins of those present here on earth. It seems that here we have an indication of the fact that there will be an administrative authority here on earth which has the ability and privilege given from the Lord to forgive or remit sins in His name. This authority was given first to Peter (Matt 16:19), then to the wider circle of the apostles (John 20), and lastly it was given to those who would make up the nucleus of the Church to be formed (Matt 18:18; 2 Cor 2:4–8).

The results of the preaching

In Matthew's Gospel it is assumed that nobody will refuse to be baptised. The fact of believing is not mentioned, although of course it is supposed to be included. Another interesting thing that is not mentioned is the Ascension, but we do have the promise that the Lord Jesus, the Messiah, would remain with the believing remnant of Israel '...until the completion of the age'.

Summarising what we have discovered about the Great Commission as described in all the four gospels, we see that it does not in every and each case have either the same contents or the same aim in view. The commission as recorded by Matthew has never yet been fulfilled literally. It will be taken up and completed by the believing remnant of Israel in the future, after the Church has been taken away out of this world, and during the Great Tribulation, which is also called 'the time of Jacob's trouble' (indicating that it is the time of Israel's tribulation, not the Church's), and in preparation for the coming King. The execution of the commission as described by Luke has already been begun. We read about this in the Acts of the Apostles. The Lord had said in Luke 24:47 'And that repentance and remission of sins should be preached in his name among all nations, beginning at Jerusalem.' As this commission has not yet been completed, it remains the literal and specific commission which the Lord has given to all of us Christians who live in the period between Pentecost and the second coming of Christ (the rapture of the Church).

We see then that the commission is also addressed to you and me: to us all! We must go forth therefore with the good news of Christ the Saviour of the world, and speak of Him everywhere in the power which the Holy Spirit gives, for we are sent by the Lord Himself. We must make a start with obeying this commission of preaching this good news, by lip and by life, just where we find ourselves at this very moment. We must preach the gospel without distinction to all peoples. The Lord Himself will confirm His word with power, but that is not something we ought to occupy ourselves with. Our task is simply to witness, to testify, to preach and to sow the good seed of the gospel. The Lord will occupy Himself personally with the results and growth and the salvation of souls. We are only channels, who pass on this message of grace. We must preach repentance, forgiveness and peace with God.

After this present period of grace, that is the period in which the Church is here on earth, (but she will one day be taken away as the Bride of Christ to be with Him in heaven), others, that is to say, converted and believing Jews will continue the preaching. Their preaching has a different character from the gospel of grace. It is rather a message that proclaims the soon appearing on the world scene of the promised King who will come to establish His thousand years' kingdom on earth. This preaching, you will recall, was begun by John the Baptist. After his death it was continued by the Lord Jesus Christ and His disciples, but interrupted by the crucifixion of the King. As we have seen, it will be taken up again and preached after the interim period of the Church, already lasting almost 2000 years, has come to an end. The contents of the Gospel of the Kingdom are first to make disciples of all men; second to baptise and third to teach.

Do we now have to draw the conclusion that evangelisation is the task of the Church as such, or that to evangelise is the first and foremost task of the believers? Do we all have to abandon our daily occupations, jobs and professions, and start evangelising in the home-land and abroad? Are we all evangelists, and have we all received the gift of an evangelist? The answer of course is obvious. The Church's task here on earth in the first place is to make known the manifest wisdom of God (Eph 3:10) and she is called the pillar and base of the truth (1 Tim 3:15). She in herself is not the truth, nor does the Church as such evangelise, but she has within her those who have the gift of an evangelist.

What then is more important, to evangelise or to maintain sound doctrine? We begin by saying that they are in any case never mutually exclusive! We must be careful to 'rightly divide the word of truth' (2 Tim 2:15). It is a human weakness to swing the pendulum, and to lose a scriptural balance. Perish the thought that sects and denominations and the multiple divisions in the Church of God are a means by which the manifold truth of Christ is preached! There is only *one* true Church here on earth, which is made up of all true, born again believers in whom dwells the Holy Spirit. The Church's task here on earth is not one-sided. Believers who gather in localities on the basis of the unity of the one, universal body of Christ must watch against one-sidedness: not only doctrine, not exclusively gospel preaching. It must not be the one at the expense of the other, or the one more than the other.

We read in Ephesians 4:11,12; 'And he (Jesus Christ) gave some, apostles; and some, prophets; and some, evangelists; and some, pastors and teachers for the perfecting of the saints, for the work of the ministry, for the edifying of the body of Christ". Neither the gift of an evangelist, nor that of pastor and teacher is given to all believers. But this fact does not mean that those of us who are not gifted in this way must remain inactive. We should all as much as possible seek to influence and reach out for the souls around us to come to Christ and show them that we love them for Christ's sake. All believers should have a big, large heart for the spreading and preaching of the gospel. A brother once said: 'If I lived close enough to Him, I would not be able to pass a sinner without telling him of the Saviour, and I could not pass a fellow-believer without sharing with him Christ, who is his life in heaven'.

Our first duty therefore is not to go out and preach the gospel, but quite simply to do what He personally charges us with, and this may differ from person to person. Some have the gift of teaching and not that of an evangelist. Does this mean that the teacher is therefore never concerned about lost sinners? Would he never pray for the salvation of souls? Would he not encourage and support the preaching of the gospel? Of course not! We could not imagine such a thing for a moment. The Lord Jesus would certainly never approve of such an attitude.

It is tragic and very unfortunate however that it sometimes happens that there is no happy unity and cooperation between two believers who exercise the gift of teacher and evangelist, but rather they oppose one another. No doubt this must grieve the Lord terribly, and it is in direct contradiction to the law that operates in the Body of Christ as described in 1 Corinthians 12.

To speak of Christ, or to give one's testimony of what the Lord has done for one, is of course different from having the gift and calling of an evanglist. The Lord uses us in that work which He commits to each one of us personally. The teacher will occupy himself with the exposition and clarifying of God's word, and would seem therefore to be more concerned with imparting truth than with persons. The evangelist and pastor would perhaps be more concerned with the personality of those with whom they come in contact. Timothy may not have received the gift of an evangelist, but Paul tells him nevertheless: 'Do the work of an evangelist' (2 Tim 4:5). Alternatively the verse may simply indicate that one could become so occupied with imparting doctrine, or get bogged down with troubles amongst believers, that the duty to evangelise is quite forgotten. But notice that Paul also says: 'preach the word' (v.2). This seems to indicate that we must always seek to maintain the right scriptural balance and preach the counsel of God!

In conclusion, we have seen that the call of the Lord Jesus is addressed to all believers without distinction: 'come, follow me'. As we follow Him day by day, we speak of Him and do the work of an evangelist, because we love the Saviour and we love lost sinners as He loves them. but we also distinguish the special call of the Lord, which is related to the exercise of a special gift which a believer has received from the Lord. But the golden rule seems to me that when we see a man drowning and we know how to swim and save him, we do not need any special command in order to jump into the water and save him before it is too late. In this sense the need does constitute the call!

8

HOW DO I KNOW THAT I'M CALLED?

Perhaps some of us are still not sure whether it is we who are meant. Some of us may be invalids, or totally incapacitated, or old and unable to do much. Are we also called? How do we know?

A call is very personal

God's methods are not stereo-typed; He does not deal with all of us in the same way, but in a very personal way, for He knows us better than we know ourselves. Of course we can learn a great deal from the experiences of others, how they realised the Lord's call, but we should not try to copy them. Scripture says we should seek to imitate their faith (Heb 13:7). The Lord uses a very great variety of ways in dealing with his children. They are all very special to Him. You and I are special to Him and therefore He will use ways with you and me which are exactly suited to our particular make-up.

Philip was called to serve in Samaria. But it seems that God used widespread persecutions to scatter His children so they would preach the gospel everywhere, rather than staying at Jerusalem (see Acts 8:4,5). Later he was directed by an angel to go towards the desert, and there the Holy Spirit told him to join himself to the Ethiopian eunuch in his chariot.

The apostle Paul was forbidden by the Holy Spirit to travel in a certain direction, but the same Spirit also guided him next into another direction. The ultimate step which led him to Rome to continue his ministry there was evidently not exactly by a special revelation (although the fact that he would witness at Rome was revealed to him, but not the exact moment of time).

Isaiah had a vision of the glory of Jahweh and His greatness and majesty. He became overwhelmingly aware of his own corruption as a believer. This indwelling corruption is called 'the sin that dwells in me' in Romans 7. After one of the seraphim had flown to him with a live coal from off the altar and therewith touched his lips, and so in a figurative way purified him, he became conscious of being in the very presence of God. And so it was that he became a listener to a conversation in the Godhead: 'Whom shall I send, and who will go for us?'. Isaiah's immediate response was: 'Here am I, send me' (Is 6:5–8).

Abraham said: 'Behold, here I am' (Gen 22:1), and Ananias likewise responded with : 'Behold, I am here, Lord' (Acts 9:10). All these men lived in close fellowship with the Lord and were thus able and ready to respond at once to the desire of their Lord and Master. It is similar to a call to the sea in the case of a sailor, or the call to the Himalayas of the mountaineer, or the call of adventure. You just cannot explain it. Only those who are as it were tuned to the right wave-length, will hear the voice of the One who calls them, and they will respond wholeheartedly.

It is not mechanical

Do you really want to know His will for your life? Are you looking for guidance to know what the Lord wants you to do, today or with a view to the future? Do not be like that believer who looked for guidance through the reading of his Bible. He had a problem, and so he took his Bible in his hands, closed his eyes piously, and then thrust his finger between the pages. Opening his eyes and the Bible, he read the following verse: '(Judas) ...went and hanged himself' (Matt 27:5). 'No', he thought, 'this definitely is not what I am looking for.' So he tried a second time. Again he closed his eyes, opened the Bible and fixed his finger on a certain place. Now he read: 'Go, and do thou likewise' (Luke 10:37). You get the meaning, don't you? This is a completely wrong and unworthy way to read the Bible, or to seek daily guidance.

The prophet Elijah expected to hear the voice of God's guidance in a terrific storm, a strong wind which rent the mountains, and broke the rocks in pieces. Something really spectacular! There are believers who also expect to be called by the Lord in a similarly mysterious and spectacular manner. They imagine they will hear a loud voice in the middle of the night telling them dramatically: 'You must go for me to Zaire'. But no! In the case of Elijah it was not through the storm that God spoke to him. Perhaps it was in the earth-quake which followed next? Or perhaps in the fire? But no! In neither of these two spectacular miracles did the Lord come to him. It was in a still small voice, hardly audible!

What are you waiting for, my brother and sister, who read these pages? Ever since you received Christ as your own personal Saviour He has been calling you, saying: 'Come, follow Me'. Have you not heard His voice? Are you still waiting for a miracle to happen, some spectacular event, a voice in the night, calling you? Perhaps you say: 'Yes, I am willing to follow Him, but I am not sure that He has called me'. Please do like Elijah, and listen to His gentle voice which calls you now. Yes, He calls *you* now! He calls you to complete surrender. He calls you to follow Him alone. Nothing else, nothing more. Faith accepts His gentle leading. Only unbelief still hesitates and insists on a miracle happening.

'And He said unto another, follow me...' (Luke 9:59). Perhaps in the past you have heard His voice. But your answer, even although you have never audibly expressed it, has been in fact like this man in v.59: 'Lord...me first'. But that is an absolute contradiction in terms. Dare we say in one breath 'LORD' and at same time maintain ourselves and insist upon our own rights, saying, or rather acting: *me first*. We have had to make a choice the moment His call was heard. We did make the choice: 'I...not Christ.' Is that what you did then? Oh, yes, we are believers – but we are not disciples of Jesus Christ; we prefer to follow our own way.

But it is not yet too late to change direction. The Lord Jesus does not compel you. He simply appeals to your affections. The Spirit of God in us yearns with deep desire for us to be all for the Lord Jesus. That our response is: *Not I, but Christ*. Remember, we are not here discussing that special call to a service, but the call to discipleship. It is possible, when first we have responded to this call to follow Him, subsequently He may call us to follow Him to a service He has for us to do, whether at home or abroad. But let us get the order right.

To be occupied with Him, to yield utterly to Him, to let Him have His own way with us, comes first. Not service! That is only an outflow, a result of our basic relationship with Christ.

Hearing this call is in fact the moment in which the believer realises that he is identified, one with Christ. Dead, buried, raised, seated with and in Him! from this position of our being one with Him, everything in our daily lives is going to be dominated. It is therefore impossible to imagine the call of Christ to you and me as something separate, and unrelated to a life of close fellowship and communion with Him.

It is not visionary

God deals with us in clear daylight, so to speak! He can of course, use a dream, or a vision to reveal His will. He often used this method in the past when there was no written revelation of Himself, no Old or New Testament, and no completed canon of scripture.

We refer once more to the vision Paul saw. (Acts 16:9). Let us note well that his vision was given him after he had been a very active worker for the Lord; he was now on his second missionary journey. This vision was therefore simply a link, a small detail, in the guidance he was in need of. He had been obedient in his total surrender to Christ. This was basic for Paul. You cannot receive guidance unless you have been obedient first of all to this basic call to surrender. Now, Paul needed further direction in a very special circumstance. He had made it his habit always to act in obedience to God's word. That is the reason why he stopped immediately the moment he became aware in his spirit that the Holy Spirit did not want him to proceed in a different direction.

There was this certain awareness in Paul's spirit. A radio transmitter station sends out news on a certain wave-length or frequency: only a receiver tuned to the same frequency will hear the voice of the announcer. This is similar to the awareness a spiritual believer feels when His Master speaks to him. Everything which hinders the reception and the hearing of His voice must be put out of our lives. Then we will be open and receptive to His voice. This is difficult to describe; it has to be experienced. It is like dying embers being suddenly re-kindled. The smouldering embers of our inner spiritual lives were almost extinguished. But then the Holy Spirit of God came and breathed a revival in our hearts. God's Spirit showed us the will of the Lord: 'Follow Me'. Our total being suddenly went out to Him as never before. The almost extinguished fire-glow of our affections and love for Him was transformed into a blazing flame through the breath of God's Spirit. A deep and over-whelming consciousness that Christ is calling us to Him-self now floods our entire being (Phil 3:12). We hear Him say to us: 'Ye have not chosen me, but I have chosen you, and ordained you, that ye should go and bring forth fruit, and that your fruit should remain'. (John 15:16).

His call must find an echo in our hearts

It cannot be otherwise, but our hearts now throb in deep response, overflowing in praise and worship and total abandon, perhaps in the words of this hymn:

> Have I an object, Lord, below,
>   Which would divide my heart from Thee:
> Which would divert its even flow
>   In answer to Thy constancy?
> Oh, teach me quickly to return,
>   And cause my heart afresh to burn!
>
> Be Thou the object bright and fair
>   To fill and satisfy the heart:
> My hope to meet Thee in the air,
>   And never more from Thee to part.
> That I may undistracted be
>   To follow, serve, and wait for Thee.

We will now discover that doing His will is like heaven on earth. 'I must have the Saviour with me, for I dare not walk alone. I must feel His presence near me, and His arm around me thrown,', will be our daily motto. Does He tell me to stay where I am right now, and to keep on doing what I am doing? That is enough for me. Does He want me away from home, from my own country? He will lead me all the way. That is my joy! Does He give me a hidden and inconspicuous service to do for Him? Or is it a public service? His name be eternally praised!

   'HERE AM I, LORD'.

Further Recommended Reading

THE WATCHING SERVANT
24pp   John Nelson Darby
a powerful sermon on Christ's coming again.

OPERATION WORLD
a handbook for World Intercession.
272pp   P. J. Johnstone
STL. Bromley, Kent.

THE GOLDEN THREAD
The Diary of a missionary to China.
167pp   Elsie Koll
Introduction by Cor Bruins.

THE GREAT COMMISSION
96pp   C. H. Mackintosh

PAPERS ON EVANGELIZATION
86pp   C. H. Mackintosh
Continuously in print for over a century!

A PATTERN IN THE HEAVENS
Missionary service in Egypt
155pp   Regina E. Pearson 1985

INCIDENTS IN GOSPEL WORK
The way the Lord led me.
118pp   Charles Stanley
Continuously in print for over a century!

*Available from your local Christian bookshop or in
case of difficulty from the publishers.*

Other
CHAPTER TWO
Publications

John Blackburn	The True Worship
E.N.C.	Christians gathered in the Name of the Lord Jesus
Edward Dennett	Three addresses on the Lord's Coming
C. H. Mackintosh	Holy Brethren, their title and their work Jehoshaphat Remnant, Past and Present The Three Appearings
A. J. Pollock	The Fellowship to which all Christians are called
John Rouw	Gems tell their Secret House of Gold (available in counter display boxes of 12) Shalom and Israel
Hamilton Smith	The Book of Ruth
B. & S. Warnes	Read it daily, study notes on Mark's Gospel

'Quality books in an age of change'

Available from your local Christian bookshop or in case of difficulty from the publishers.